The UK Ninja Foodi
Cookbook with Pictures

Easy, Affordable, and Delicious Ninja Foodi Recipes for Beginners to
Cook with Ninja Foodi SmartLid Multi-Cooker & MAX Multi-Cooker

Janice Sottile

TABLE OF CONTENTS

4

Introduction

Just when you think that Ninja Foodi can't amaze you with any more of its innovation, the company releases an amazing product to surprise you with its latest kitchen technology. Yes, Ninja Foodi has managed to again dazzle its customers with yet another kitchen miracle, which has made pressure cooking, baking, air frying, steam crisp, sous vide, dehydrating, and broiling easier than ever before. The Ninja Foodi Smart XL Pressure Cooker Steam Fryer is the innovation of today that has successfully brought a variety of cooking functions into a single appliance. Imagine, instead of having a steamer, crisper, air fryer, and an oven separately lying on your kitchen shelf, you will have one single appliance which can do all of that with much efficiency. This 14-in-1 multipurpose Ninja Foodi Smart XL Steam Air Fryer is extremely user-friendly and gives its users complete control over both the cooking time and temperature. This Ninja Foodi Steam Air Fryer cookbook is designed to introduce all its readers to this digital pressure cooker, its features, and its better use. There is a range of recipes all cooked in an air fry oven, accompanied by a 21 days meal plan for all beginners.

Fundamentals of Ninja Foodi Smart XL Pressure Cooker Steam Fryer

What is Ninja Foodi Smart XL Pressure Cooker Steam Fryer?

The newest electric pressure cooker designed by Shark Ninja is the 14-in-one Ninja Foodi Smart XL Pressure Cooker Steam Air Fryer. There is presently only an 8-quart size available. A ceramic cooking pot, a cook-and-crisp basket, and a reversible rack are all included in the box. With an extra-large, family-sized capacity and the ability to pressure cook, air fry, and Steam Crisp all under one Smart Lid, the Ninja Foodi Smart XL Pressure Cooker Steam Fryer is able to do all the cooking for you. With this smart lid's sliding feature, you can access all 14 cooking settings and 3 cooking modes from one lid.

Benefits of Using Ninja Foodi Smart XL Pressure Cooker Steam Fryer

The device has a touchscreen and dial combination, which makes the control panel look neater and make it simpler to use. In other words, it lacks the confusing number of buttons that prior models do. Additionally, the slider makes switching between settings simple (which also neatly organizes the cooking functions). The "smart" apps' trademark default settings also remove the element of guesswork for a simpler experience. The smart lid enhances both your recipes and the machine's overall usability. There are separate lids on another pressure cooker/air fryer combination. You must pressure cook and air fry separately to replicate steam frying. You don't even need to swap out the cover with the Ninja Foodi Smart XL Pressure Cooker Steam Fryer, and you can utilize both the steam and air fry functions. The majority of cooking features are self-explanatory. It functions, in essence, like a convection oven with a powerful fan and great air circulation for consistent cooking. More importantly, you may have healthier and less expensive fried dishes because you just require little to no oil (compared to deep-frying). Second, the Ninja Foodi Smart XL Pressure Cooker Steam Fryer can be used as a proofer. In essence, this equipment makes baking simpler because you can control the temperature and time. Additionally, after proving, you can use the steam directly to bake rather than moving it around. There will be less cleanup to do later. (Applicable to the sear/sauté function as well.) The sous vide program is also available in this cooker. By doing this, you may make the inexpensive meals taste more upscale.

Cooking Functions and Features

It has great flexibility and toughness. In comparison to other cooking techniques, it cooks food much faster. As an environment fryer, it also cooks food without the need for oil, resulting in lower-calorie and healthier meals. Ninja Foodi Smart XL Pressure Cooker Steam Fryer has all these cooking features that you can use with the help of user-friendly control.

• Pressure: Keep food soft while cooking it quickly.
• Steam & crisp: Create one-touch whole meals, juicy and crisp vegetables and proteins, and handmade artisan bread with Steam & Crisp.
• Steam & bake: Quickly and with less fat, bake fluffier cakes and quick bread.
• Air fry: With little to no oil, air frying adds crispness and snap to food.
• Broil: To caramelize and brown the tops of your meal, use strong heat coming from above.
• Bake/roast: Use the appliance as an oven for a variety of baked goods, tender meats, and more.
• Dehydrate: Dehydrate fruits, vegetables, and meats for wholesome snacking.
• Proof: Provide a space for the dough to rest and rise.
• Sear/sauté: Use the device as a cooktop to cook a variety of foods, including meats, vegetables, and sauces.
• Steam: Cook delicate items at a high temperature while using steam.
• Sous vide: Sous vide, which is French for "under vacuum," is a feature that uses a precisely controlled water bath to slowly cook food that is sealed in a plastic bag.
• Slow cook: Cook your meal for a longer amount of time at a lower temperature.
• Yogurt: Pasteurize milk and allow it to ferment to make creamy homemade yogurt.
• Keep warm: The appliance will switch to keep warm at the conclusion of the cycle when steam, slow cooking, or pressure is being used. Once the function has begun, press the keep warm button to stop the automated transition.

Operation Keys

• Smart lid slider: As you slide the slider, the features that are available in each mode will light up.
• Dial: Use the dial to cycle among the available functions once you've selected a mode using the slider until your desired function is highlighted.
• Left arrows: To change the cooking temperature, use the "up/down" keys to the left of the display.
• Right arrows: To change the cooking time, press the "up/down" keys next to the display.
• Hit the "start/stop" button to begin cooking. The current cooking function will be stopped if the button is pressed while the appliance is cooking.
• Power: The power button turns off the appliance and ends all cooking settings.

Ninja Smart XL Steam Fryer OL 601 Vs OL 701

Ninja Foodi Smart XL Pressure Cooker Steam Fryer is mainly available in two different variations, the OL 600 series and the OL 700 series. Since I have personally used the OL601 and OL701 versions I will draw a little comparison of those two models to help you decide which one to bring home. First of all, if you choose the OL701 over the OL601, you won't lose any functionality because the OL701 has the same appearance, accessories, and features as the OL601. When using any mode that requires water, which is most of them, water will drip from the lid to the counter on both models.

The pressure release on the OL601 is the same as it was on earlier models. By adjusting the valve, you can release pressure slowly or quickly. You can digitally select the release you want on the OL701. Natural Release is the cooker's default setting, but you can also select Quick Release or Delayed Release, and it will be carried out automatically. This doesn't bother me personally because I don't mind opening the valve quickly to relieve pressure or allowing the cooker naturally release for around 10 minutes before opening the pressure release valve to release any remaining pressure.

Unlike the OL601, which lacks a probe, the OL701 has a probe that connects to the underside of the lid. This is the OL701's main selling factor in my opinion. They refer to the "Smart Cooking" feature of the OL701. The pressure cooker's side has a holder for the probe. You can select the meat, poultry, or fish you're cooking using the probe and choose a preset temperature or manually set it. This, in my opinion, is the OL701's greatest advantage.

When pressure cooking, it's usually preferable to hazard a guess as to when the meat will be the required doneness and temperature. You may pressure cook roasts, chicken, etc. to the desired internal temperature using the probe. You can select beef, pig, or chicken in the pressure cooking mode for presets, and you can also select between well and shred. You can specify the internal temperature at which the meat should be cooked if you select manually. The guidebook provides temperature recommendations for various levels of doneness and permits carryover cooking. You can select presets for beef, chicken, pig, and fish in the steam and crisp mode, as well as your preferred level of doneness (rare, med. rare, medium, medium well, and well). For a manual setting, you can choose the preferred temperature. The steam and bake mode does not support the probe.

Step-By-Step Ninja Foodi Smart XL Pressure Cooker Steam Fryer

Take off and throw away any packaging, stickers, and tape from the appliance. Pay close attention to operational guidelines, precautions, and warnings to prevent harm or property damage. Warm, soapy water should be used to wash the silicone ring, removable cooking pot, Cook & Crisp Basket, deluxe reversible rack, and condensation collector. Rinse and dry everything well afterwards. NEVER use a dishwasher to clean the cooker base.

The silicone ring can be put in either direction and is reversible. On the underside of the lid, insert the silicone ring around the outside of the silicone ring rack. Make certain it is completely inserted and flatly rests beneath the silicone ring rack. High (Hi) pressure will be the unit's default setting. To change the time to 2 minutes, press the right-down arrow. To start, hit the "start/stop". The progress bars and the letter "PrE" on this display signal that the device is developing pressure. The timer starts to tick when the device is fully pressurized.

The appliance will beep and show "End" when the cooking time has expired before manually quickly releasing the pressured steam. When the pressure release valve is about to open, a warning bell will ring. Steam will flow from the pressure release valve as it opens. Slide the slider towards the right side to open the lid once the display says "OPN Lid." Next, remove the cover. Depending on the amount, temperature, and chosen pressure level of the materials, the time to pressure will change.

Water Test

It is advised that new users perform a water test to get comfortable with pressure cooking. 3 cups of room temperature water should be added to the pot before placing it in the cooker base. Close the lid and slide the lever to PRESSURE. Ensure that the seal position is selected on the pressure release valve.

Natural Pressure Release VS. Quick Pressure Release

Natural Pressure Release: As the appliance cools down after pressure cooking is finished, steam will naturally escape from it. Depending on the volume of liquid and food in the pot, this could take up to 20 minutes or longer. The appliance will enter Keep Warm mode during this period. If you want to exit Keep Warm mode, press the

KEEP WARM button. The display will read "OPN Lid" when the unit has finished its natural pressure release. Only use a quick pressure release if your recipe specifies it. Rotate the pressure release valve handle to the VENT position to immediately release pressure via the valve once pressure cooking is done and the keep warm light is on. Some steam will still be present in the appliance after pressure has been released naturally or by using the pressure release valve; this steam will escape when the lid is opened.

Steps for Pressure Cooking

The control panel display will show PrE and progress bars as the pressure inside the unit increases. The liquid in the pot, the number of components, and their temperature all affect how long it takes to reach pressure. The lid will lock for safety as the unit builds pressure and will unlock as the pressure is released. Cooking will start once the appliance reaches full pressure, and the timer will start to clock down.

Press the button after inserting the power cord into a wall outlet to turn on the device. Fill the pot with the ingredients, at least 1 cup of liquid, and any other required equipment. Past the PRESSURE MAX line, DO NOT continue to fill the pot. Put the lid on. The pressure release valve is then turned to the SEAL position. The slider moved to PRESSURE. To choose Hi or LO, use the "up and down" keys to the left of the display.

To change the cooking time, move the "up and down" keys to the right of the display in one-minute increments up to 1 hour, then for 1 hour to 4 hours you can increase the value in 5-minute increments. To start or stop cooking, hit the "start/stop". Pressure will start to build in the unit. "PrE" and progress bars will be seen on the display. When the appliance is fully pressurized, the timer will start to run out.

Rotate the pressure release valve to the VENT position when the cooking time reaches zero minutes. The device will beep, go into Keep

Warm mode automatically, and start counting down. It has depressurized when the device shows "OPN Lid," at which point you can adjust the slider towards the right side to open the lid.

Steps for Steam & Crisp

Add the ingredients as directed by the recipe instructions. Now move the Slider to Steam & Crisp. Steam & Crisp will be the default choice for the function. The time and temperature settings will automatically display. Use the "up and down" keys to the left of the display to select a temperature between 300°F and 450°F in 5-degree increments. The cook time can be changed using the "up and down" keys to the right of the display in minute increments up to an hour.

Hit the "start/stop" to start or stop cooking. The progress bars and "PrE" indicator on the LCD demonstrate that the device is generating steam. The number of ingredients in the pot determines how long it will take to steam. The display panel will show the set temperature and the timer will start counting down when the unit reaches the proper steam level. The appliance will beep and display "End" for five minutes when the cooking time reaches zero. Use the "Up" key to the right of the display to add more time if your cuisine needs it. The appliance will not pre-heat.

Steps for Steam & Bake

Set the multipurpose pan in the lower position on the rack. After that, insert the rack and accessories into the pot. Move the slider to Steam & Crisp, then choose Steam & Bake with the dial. It will show the current temperature setting. With the "up and down" keys to the left of the display, you can select a temperature between 225°F and 400°F in 5-degree increments. The cook time can be changed in one-minute increments up to one hour and fifteen minutes by using the "up and down" keys to the right of the display. Hit the "start/stop" to start the stove. As the unit builds steam, the display panel will show "PrE" and progress bars. It takes 20 minutes to steam.

The temperature will be displayed on the display and the timer will start to count down after pre-heating is finished. The appliance will beep and display "End" for five minutes when the cooking time reaches zero. Use the "Up" key to the right of the display to add more time if your cuisine needs it. The appliance will not pre-heat.

Steps for Air Frying

The Cook & Crisp Basket or the premium reversible rack should be placed in the pot. A diffuser ought to be fastened to the basket. Ingredients can be added to the Deluxe Reversible Rack or Cook & Crisp Basket. Put the lid on. The slider should be set to AIR FRY/STOVETOP; AIR FRY will be selected by default. It will show the current temperature setting. With the "up and down" keys to the left of the display, select a temperature between 300°F and 400°F in 5-degree increments.

In order to change the cooking time in one-minute increments up to an hour, use the "up and down" keys to the right of the display. Hit the "start/stop" to start the stove. The device will beep and "End" will flash three times on the display when the cooking time reaches zero.

Steps for Broiling

Alternatively, you can follow the instructions in your recipe and place the premium reversible rack in the pot on the higher broil setting. Arrange the ingredients on the rack, then cover. The slider should be set to AIR FRY/STOVETOP, and the dial should be set to BROIL. Adjust the cooking time up to 30 minutes using the "up and down" keys on the right side of the display. To start or stop cooking, hit the "start/stop". The device will beep and "End" will flash three times on the display when the cooking time reaches zero.

Steps for Baking or Roasting

Add any necessary ingredients and accessories to the pot. Put the lid on. The slider should be set to AIR FRY/STOVETOP, then BAKE/ROAST should be chosen with the dial. It will show the current temperature setting. With the "up and down" keys to the left of the display, you may select a temperature between 250°F and 400°F in 5-degree increments. The cook time can be changed by using the "up and down" keys to the right of the display in minute increments up to 1 hour. To start or stop cooking, hit the "START/STOP". The device will beep and "End" will flash three times on the display when the cooking time reaches zero.

Steps for Dehydrating

Lower the deluxe reversible rack into the pot, then arrange some ingredients on top of the rack. Lay the deluxe layer over the reversible rack as shown below, holding it by its handles. Then top the deluxe layer with a layer of ingredients and secure the lid. The slider should be moved to AIR FRY/STOVETOP, then select DEHYDRATE on the dial. It will show the current temperature setting. With the "up and down" keys to the left of the display, you can select a temperature between 80°F and 195°F in 5-degree increments.

To change the cooking time from one hour to twelve hours, use the "up and down" keys to the right of the display. To start or stop cooking, hit the "START/STOP". The device will beep and "End" will flash three times on the display when the cooking time reaches zero.

Steps fot Sear/Sauté

Fill the pot inside the Ninja Foodi Smart XL Pressure Cooker Steam Fryer with the ingredients. Open the lid or move the slider to AIR FRY/STOVETOP, then with the help of the dial select Sear/Sauté. It will show the current temperature setting. To choose "Lo1," "2," "3," "4", or "Hi5", use the "up and down" keys to the left of the display. To start or stop cooking, hit the "Start/Stop".

To switch off the Sear/Sauté feature, hit the "start/stop". Hit the "start/stop" to stop the current cooking function, then with the help of the slider and dial pick the next function you want to use. When using a cooking pot, ALWAYS use non-stick utensils. A nonstick coating on the pot will be scratched if metal utensils are used.

NOTE: For "4" and "Hi5", Sear/Sauté will automatically shut off after an hour, and for "LO1," "2," and "3," it will do so after four hours.

How to Proof a Dough?

Add the dough and secure the lid of the pot or Air Fry Basket. The slider should be set to AIR FRY/STOVETOP, then PROOF should be chosen using the dial. It will show the current temperature setting. The temperature ranges from 75°F to 95°F, and you may adjust it in 5-degree increments by using the "up and down" keys to the left of the display. To change the proof time between 20 minutes and 2 hours, use the "up and down" keys to the right of the display. To start or stop cooking, hit the "START/STOP". The device will beep and "End" will flash three times on the display when the cooking time reaches zero.

Tips for Using Accessories

Besides the 14 amazing cooking functions, what makes this steam fryer special are the different accessories that come along with it. You can use those accessories to cook all sorts of food. Here is how you can use its accessories:

Deluxe Reversible Rack

Set the Deluxe Reversible Rack's bottom layer in the lowest position. Put the ingredients on the rack's lowest layer. The Deluxe layer should then be slid through the handles of the bottom layer. Add the remaining ingredients to the Deluxe layer to enhance the amount of food you can prepare.

Cook & Crisp Basket

Pull the two diffuser fins out of the groove on the basket to remove the diffuser for cleaning. Then, firmly pull the diffuser down. Place the Cook & Crisp Basket on top of the diffuser and firmly press down.

The Smart Lid with Slider

You may switch between cooking modes by using the slider, which also notifies the lid of your current function.
- Pressure
- Steam Crisp
- Air Fry/Stovetop

To open and close the lid, always use the handle that is situated above the slider. When the slider is set to Steam & Crisp or AIR FRY/STOVETOP, you can open and close the lid. The lid cannot be opened when the slider is in the PRESSURE position. Slide the slider to the "Steam & Crisp" or "AIR FRY/STOVETOP" position to open the device if there is no pressure within.

The Anti-Clog Cap

The anti-clog cap shields users from potential food splatters and prevents the inner valve of the lid from clogging. After each use, it should be cleaned using a cleaning brush. Holding the anti-clog cap between your thumb and bent index finger, turn your wrist in a clockwise direction to remove it. Put it in place and press down to reinstall. Before operating the device, check if the anti-clog cap is in the proper position.

Ensure the silicone ring is securely mounted in the ring's grove and the anti-clog cap is securely fastened to the pressure release valve before each usage. After cooking, be sure to remove any extra water that accumulated in the condensation collector. This collector can only be used with a silicone ring made specifically for Ninja Foodi Smart Lid models. No other Ninja Foodi silicone rings or rings made by other companies may be worn.

Special Tips to Use Ninja Foodi Smart XL Pressure Cooker Steam Fryer

Make sure the ingredients are layered evenly and without overlap in the cooking pot for uniform browning. Make sure to shake halfway through the designated cook time if the ingredients overlap. I advise first wrapping smaller items in a parchment paper or foil pouch if they might fall through the premium reversible rack. After cooking, keep food at a warm mode, safe temperature by using the Keep Warm option. I advise keeping the lid on and using this feature right before serving to avoid food drying out. Use the Reheat function to reheat food.

Cleaning

After each usage, the appliance needs to be completely cleaned. Before cleaning, unplug the appliance from the wall outlet. Use a moist towel to clean the control panel and the base of the stove. The Cook & Crisp Basket, detachable diffuser, luxury reversible rack, silicone ring, and cooking pot can all be cleaned in the dishwasher. The anti-clog cap and pressure release valve can be cleaned with water and dish soap.

Cooking pots, deluxe reversible racks, and Cook & Crisp Baskets should be filled with water and given time to soak before being cleaned if food residue is stuck to them. AVOID using scouring pads. If scrubbing is required, use a nylon pad or brush with liquid dish soap or non-abrasive cleaner.

After each use, let all pieces air-dry. Taking off and replacing the Silicone Ring. Pull the silicone ring from the metal ring rack slowly outward, part by section. Either side of the ring can be mounted facing upward. To reinstall, carefully insert the silicone ring piece by piece into the rack while making sure the metal ring rack is visible. Remove any food particles from the silicone ring and anti-clog cap after use. To prevent odor, keep the silicone ring clean.

Odors can be eliminated by washing them in the dishwasher or warm, soapy water. It is however typical for it to take in the aroma of some acidic foods. It is advised to keep several silicone rings on hand. Additional silicone rings are available on ninjaaccessories.com. NEVER use too much force to remove the silicone ring, as this could damage the rack and compromise the pressure-sealing mechanism. Replace any silicone ring that has cracks, cuts, or other damage right away.

Prior to using any "wet cooking functions," such as Pressure, Steam, Sous Vide, Slow Cook, Sear/Sauté, and all Steam & Crisp functions, I advise checking the interior of the lid. I advise steam cleaning the appliance if you see any food leftover or oil buildup on the heating element or fan. After that, wipe down the interior of the lid.

Steam Cleaning

Pour about 2-3 cups of water into the pot. Move Smart Slider to AIR FRY/STOVETOP. Set the timer to 30 minutes and choose STEAM. Hit the start/stop button. Use a lightly damp cloth or sponge to clean the interior of the lid once the clock hits zero and the device has cooled. WARNING: Avoid touching the fan when cleaning the inside of the lid.

Frequently Asked Questions & Notes

Why does it take my unit so long to reach pressure? How long does it take for pressure to build?

Depending on the chosen temperature, the cooking pot's current temperature, and the temperature or quantity of the contents, cooking times may vary. Verify that the silicone ring is flush with the lid and fully seated. If placed properly, you should be able to rotate the ring by giving it a small tug. When pressure cooking, make sure the lid is completely secured and the pressure release valve is in the "SEAL" position. If there is not enough liquid, the unit won't pressurize.

Why does the clock go so slowly?

Instead of setting minutes, you might have done such. When adjusting the time, the display will read HH: MM and the time will change in minute steps.

How will I know when the machine starts to pressurize?

To show that the unit is developing pressure, a progress bar will load as the building animation plays. When employing the Pressure, Steam, or any other Steam & Crisp function, "PrE" and moving lights appear on the display screen.

When utilizing STEAM or PRESSURE, this shows that the unit is preheating or creating pressure. Your designated cook time will start to run out once the machine has finished creating pressure. When activating the Steam function, the appliance emits a lot of steam. When cooking, steam should normally escape through the pressure release valve.

Why am I unable to lift the lid after pressuring?

As a security measure, the lid won't open until the appliance has entirely lost pressure. To quickly discharge the pressurized steam, rotate the pressure release valve to the VENT position. Steam will suddenly erupt from the pressure release valve. The apparatus will be prepared to open once all of the steam has been discharged. Is a loose pressure release valve normal? Yes. The loose fit of the pressure release valve is deliberate; it makes it simple to switch from SEAL to VENT and helps regulate pressure by releasing a tiny quantity of steam while cooking to produce excellent results. For pressure cooking, please check to see if it is turned completely towards the SEAL position, and for quick releasing, check to see if it is turned completely towards the VENT position. The appliance hisses and cannot build pressure.

A pressure release valve should be turned to the SEAL setting, so double-check this. When you've done this and the silicone ring is still making a loud hissing noise, it might not be entirely in place. To halt cooking, hit the "start/stop", then VENT if necessary, then open the lid. Make sure the silicone ring is properly placed and flatly underneath the ring rack by applying pressure on it. Once everything is put in place, you ought to be able to rotate the ring by giving it a gentle tug. Instead of counting down, the device is counting up. The appliance is in Keep Warm mode once the cooking cycle has finished.

How much time does it take the unit to depressurize?

The amount of food in the unit and the recipe can affect how long it takes to release pressure. Unplug the appliance and wait until all the pressure has been released before opening the lid if it is taking longer than usual for the appliance to depressurize.

Troubleshooting

The error message "ADD POT" displays on the monitor. The cooker base does not contain the cooking pot. Every function requires a cooking pot.

The error message "SHUT LID" shows on the monitor. The selected function cannot begin because the lid is open.

When using the Steam or Pressure function, an "ADD WATER" error message shows on the display screen.

The water is not deep enough. To keep the device functioning, add extra water.

When using the Pressure function, a notice saying "NO PRESSURE" shows on the screen. Before starting the pressure cook cycle again, add more liquid to the cooking pot. Ensure that the seal position is selected on the pressure release valve. Verify that the silicone ring is properly fitted. The error message is displayed. The device is not operating correctly.

The error message "SLIDE" displays on the monitor. The slider should be moved to a position that corresponds to the desired cooking function.

The error message "LOCK LID" displays on the monitor. To lock the lid, slide the knob to the PRESSURE position.

4-Week Diet Plan

Week 1

Day 1:
Breakfast: Ninja Foodi Pancakes
Lunch: Italian Potatoes
Snack: Courgette Egg Tots
Dinner: Chicken Potato Stew
Dessert: Ninja Foodi Blackberry Crumble

Day 2:
Breakfast: Ninja Foodi Coconut Cereal
Lunch: Garlic Red Sweet Pepper Mix
Snack: Herbed Cauliflower Fritters
Dinner: Beef Jerky
Dessert: Rocky Road Fudge

Day 3:
Breakfast: Chorizo Omelet
Lunch: Cabbage with Carrots
Snack: Garlicky Tomato
Dinner: Ninja Foodi Salmon
Dessert: Mocha Cake

Day 4:
Breakfast: Ninja Foodi Cinnamon Tea
Lunch: Broccoli Cauliflower
Snack: Cashew Cream
Dinner: Ninja Foodi Chicken Stock
Dessert: Lemon Cheesecake

Day 5:
Breakfast: Spinach Turkey Cups
Lunch: Leeks and Carrots
Snack: Ninja Foodi Cheddar Biscuits
Dinner: Corned Beef
Dessert: Lime Blueberry Cheesecake

Day 6:
Breakfast: Fruit Pancakes
Lunch: Potatoes and Lemon Sauce
Snack: Ninja Foodi Spicy Peanuts
Dinner: Beer Battered Fish
Dessert: Chocolate Blackberry Cake

Day 7:
Breakfast: Swiss Bacon Frittata
Lunch: Okra Stew
Snack: Ninja Foodi Cod Sticks
Dinner: Chicken Saltimbocca
Dessert: Blueberry Buttermilk Cake

Week 2

Day 1:
Breakfast: Glazed Carrots
Lunch: Crispy Balsamic Cabbage
Snack: Cheese Stuffed Dates
Dinner: Bacon Strips
Dessert: Strawberry Crumble

Day 2:
Breakfast: Omelets in the Jar
Lunch: Southern Fried Cabbage with Bacon
Snack: Ninja Foodi Spicy Popcorns
Dinner: Lobster Tail
Dessert: Mini Vanilla Cheesecakes

Day 3:
Breakfast: Ninja Foodi Ham Muffins
Lunch: Minty Radishes
Snack: Ninja Foodi Spinach Chips
Dinner: Pulled Barbecue Chicken
Dessert: Honey Almond Scones

Day 4:
Breakfast: Ninja Foodi Rocket Omelet
Lunch: Low-Carb Italian Wedding Soup
Snack: Avocado Deviled Eggs
Dinner: Beef Bourguignon
Dessert: Ninja Foodi Banana Custard

Day 5:
Breakfast: Vanilla Banana Bread
Lunch: Vegetable Soup
Snack: Ninja Foodi Banana Cookies
Dinner: Butter Lime Salmon
Dessert: Ninja Foodi Yoghurt Cheesecake

Day 6:
Breakfast: Egg Bites
Lunch: Mexican Rice
Snack: Nutmeg Peanuts
Dinner: Bagel Chicken Tenders
Dessert: Double Chocolate Cake

Day 7:
Breakfast: Breakfast Oats Bowl
Lunch: Chives, Beetroot, and Carrots
Snack: Dried Tomatoes
Dinner: Adobo Steak
Dessert: Vanilla Cheesecake

Week 3

Day 1:
Breakfast: Ninja Foodi Baked Eggs
Lunch: Ninja Foodi Brown Rice
Snack: Ninja Foodi Popcorn
Dinner: Prawn Scampi Linguini
Dessert: Raspberry Cobbler

Day 2:
Breakfast: Pepperoni Omelets
Lunch: Saucy Kale
Snack: Pork Shank
Dinner: Ninja Foodi Duck Fajita Platter
Dessert: Chocolate Brownie Cake

Day 3:
Breakfast: Ninja Foodi Broccoli Pancakes
Lunch: Aubergine with Kale
Snack: Ninja Foodi Spiced Almonds
Dinner: Corned Cabbage Beef
Dessert: Chocolate Walnut Cake

Day 4:
Breakfast: Ninja Foodi Hard-boiled Eggs
Lunch: Creamy Kale
Snack: Courgette Muffins
Dinner: Ninja Foodi Broiled Mahi-Mahi
Dessert: Crispy Apple Delight

Day 5:
Breakfast: Avocado Cups
Lunch: Kale Stir Fry
Snack: Parmesan Breadsticks
Dinner: Lemon Garlic Scallops
Dessert: Mini Chocolate Cheesecakes

Day 6:
Breakfast: French Toast Bites
Lunch: Pomegranate Radish Mix
Snack: Breadsticks
Dinner: Honey Garlic Chicken
Dessert: Banana Bread

Day 7:
Breakfast: Ninja Foodi Pancakes
Lunch: Southern Fried Cabbage with Bacon
Snack: Ninja Foodi Spicy Cashews
Dinner: Crusted Pork Chops
Dessert: Air Crisped Cake

Week 4

Day 1:
Breakfast: Omelets in the Jar
Lunch: Sweet Peppers Mix
Snack: Japanese Eggs
Dinner: Gluten-free Fish Tacos
Dessert: Pineapple Chunks

Day 2:
Breakfast: Chorizo Omelet
Lunch: Courgette and Spinach Mix
Snack: Courgette Egg Tots
Dinner: Jalapeno Chicken Nachos
Dessert: Ninja Foodi Blackberry Crumble

Day 3:
Breakfast: Ninja Foodi Rocket Omelet
Lunch: Pumpkin Chili
Snack: Herbed Cauliflower Fritters
Dinner: Braised Lamb Shanks
Dessert: Rocky Road Fudge

Day 4:
Breakfast: Spinach Turkey Cups
Lunch: Black-Eyed Peas
Snack: Garlicky Tomato
Dinner: Lamb Curry
Dessert: Vanilla Cheesecake

Day 5:
Breakfast: Egg Bites
Lunch: Italian Potatoes
Snack: Cashew Cream
Dinner: Spicy Prawns
Dessert: Lime Blueberry Cheesecake

Day 6:
Breakfast: Swiss Bacon Frittata
Lunch: Garlic Red Sweet Pepper Mix
Snack: Ninja Foodi Cheddar Biscuits
Dinner: Eastern Lamb Stew
Dessert: Chocolate Walnut Cake

Day 7:
Breakfast: Glazed Carrots
Lunch: Broccoli Cauliflower
Snack: Ninja Foodi Spicy Peanuts
Dinner: Fish Skewers
Dessert: Strawberry Crumble

Chapter 1 Breakfast Recipes

Ninja Foodi Pancakes

Prep Time: 10 minutes
Cook Time: 25 minutes
Servings: 2
Ingredients:
60ml fat-free milk
½ tbsp rapeseed oil
¼ tsp ground nutmeg
30g plain flour
1 egg
2 tbsp sugar
Directions:
1. Add milk, ground nutmeg, plain flour, egg, and sugar in a large bowl. Whisk properly. 2. Pour egg mixture in the pot of Ninja Foodi and close the unit with Crisping Lid. 3. Select "Bake/Roast" function. 4. Bake for 20 minutes at 205°C/400°F and open the Crisping Lid. 5. Take out, serve and enjoy!
Nutritional Values Per Serving: Calories: 177; Fat: 5.9g; Carbs: 25.7g; Protein: 5.4g

Glazed Carrots

Prep Time: 10 minutes
Cook Time: 4 minutes
Servings: 4

Ingredients:
900g carrots, washed, peeled and sliced
Pepper, to taste
240ml water
1 tbsp butter
1 tbsp Lakanto maple syrup
Directions:
1. Add carrots and water to the cooking pot. 2. Lock and secure the Ninja Foodi with Pressure Lid, turn the pressure release valve to Seal position, then cook on "HI" pressure for 4 minutes. 3. Quick-release pressure. 4. Strain carrots. 5. Add butter and maple syrup to the warm mix, stir it gently. 6. Transfer strained carrots back to the pot and stir. 7. Coat well with maple syrup. 8. Sprinkle a bit of pepper and serve. 9. Enjoy.
Nutritional Values Per Serving: Calories: 358; Fat: 12g; Carbs: 20g; Protein: 2g

Ninja Foodi Baked Eggs

Prep Time: 12 minutes
Cook Time: 9 minutes
Servings: 3
Ingredients:
3 eggs
3 tbsp low-fat parmesan cheese, shredded
15g fresh spinach, chopped finely
3 tbsp double cream
3 tbsp olive oil
Salt and black pepper, to taste
Directions:
1. Grease three muffin tins with olive oil and add spinach in them. 2. Add in eggs and top them with double cream, parmesan cheese, salt and pepper. 3. Place the muffin tins in the pot of Ninja Foodi and select "Bake/Roast". 4. Close the Crisping Lid. 5. Bake for 9 minutes at 205°C/400°F and open the lid. 6. Take out, serve and enjoy!
Nutritional Values Per Serving: Calories: 326; Fat: 29.9g; Carbs: 2g; Protein: 15g

Ninja Foodi Coconut Cereal

Prep Time: 5 minutes
Cook Time: 8 hours 3 minutes
Servings: 3
Ingredients:
40g unsweetened coconut, shredded
240ml water
¼ tsp ground cinnamon
⅛ tsp liquid stevia
240ml unsweetened almond milk
30g coconut flour, divided
¼ tsp vanilla extract
Directions:
1. Add shredded coconut, almond milk, half of the coconut flour, water, and cinnamon in the pot of Ninja Foodi. Mix well. 2. Close the Pressure Lid and select "Slow Cook". 3. Cook on LO for 8 hours. 4. Open the lid and add in the remaining coconut flour, stevia, and vanilla extract. Mix until well combined. 5. Close the pressure lid and cook for 3 minutes. 6. Open the lid and take out. 7. Serve and enjoy!
Nutritional Values Per Serving: Calories: 102; Fat: 6.6g; Carbs: 9.6g; Protein: 2.1g

Omelets in the Jar

Prep Time: 10 minutes
Cook Time: 8 minutes
Servings: 5
Ingredients:
10 eggs
80 g double cream
75g shredded cheese

1 green pepper, chopped
1 ham steak, chopped
225g bacon, cooked and chopped
5 mason jars or other jars
Directions:
1. Grease the mason jars with rapeseed spray. 2. Whisk 2 eggs with 15g cream in a bowl then pour it into a jar. 3. Add 8g ham, green peppers, and cheese to the same jar. 4. Repeat the same steps to fill remaining jars. 5. Pour 240ml water in the Ninja Food cooking pot and place a reversible rack over it. 6. Set all the mason jars over the rack. 7. Secure the Ninja Foodi lid and turn its pressure handle to 'SEAL' position. 8. Select Pressure mode for 8 minutes at HI. 9. Once done, release the steam naturally then remove the lid. 10. Drizzle bacon and cheese over each jar. 11. Serve fresh.
Nutritional Values Per Serving: Calories 111; Total Fat 8.3 g; Total Carbs 1.9 g; Protein 7.4 g

Pepperoni Omelets

Prep Time: 10 minutes
Cook Time: 5 minutes
Servings: 4
Ingredients:
4 tbsp double cream
15 pepperoni slices
2 tbsp butter
Black pepper and salt to taste
6 whole eggs
Directions:
1. Take a suitable bowl and whisk in eggs, cream, pepperoni slices, salt, and pepper. 2. Set your Ninja Foodi to "Sear/Sauté" mode at MD and add butter and egg mix. 3. Sauté for 3 minutes, flip. 4. Lock and secure the Ninja Foodi's crisping lid and Air Crisp for 2 minutes at 175°C/350°F. 5. Transfer to a serving plate and enjoy.
Nutritional Values Per Serving: Calories: 141; Fat: 11g; Carbs: 0.6g; Protein: 9g

Chorizo Omelet

Prep Time: 10 minutes
Cook Time: 30-35 minutes
Servings: 4

Ingredients:
3 eggs, whisked
85g chorizo, chopped
30g Feta cheese, crumbled
60ml almond milk
¾ tsp chili flakes
¼ tsp salt
1 green pepper, chopped

Directions:
1. Add listed ingredients to a suitable bowl and mix well. 2. Take an omelet pan and pour the mixture on it. 3. Pre-heat your Ninja Food on "Bake/Roast" mode at a temperature of 160°C/320°F for 5 minutes. 4. Transfer the pan with omelet mix to your Ninja Foodi and cook for 30 minutes, or until the surface is golden and the egg has set properly. 5. Serve and enjoy.

Nutritional Values Per Serving: Calories: 426; Fat: 38g; Carbs: 7g; Protein: 21g

Ninja Foodi Ham Muffins

Prep Time: 10 minutes
Cook Time: 20 minutes
Servings: 4

Ingredients:
4 eggs
120g cooked ham, crumbled
75g red sweet pepper, seeded and chopped
1 tbsp water
Salt and black pepper, to taste

Directions:
1. Add eggs, salt, pepper, and water in a bowl. Mix well. 2. Now, add in red sweet pepper and crumbled ham. Mix well and set aside. 3. Pour the mixture in greased muffin-tins and place them in the pot of Ninja Foodi. 4. Select "Bake/Roast" and close the Crisping Lid. 5. Bake for 20 minutes at 175°C/350°F. 6. Take out, serve and enjoy!

Nutritional Values Per Serving: Calories: 95; Fat: 5.9g; Carbs: 2.1g; Protein: 8.5g

Ninja Foodi Broccoli Pancakes

Prep Time: 5 minutes
Cook Time: 20 minutes
Servings: 2

Ingredients:
20g chopped broccoli
30g low-fat cheddar cheese, shredded
½ tsp dried onion, minced
1 egg
½ tsp garlic powder
Salt and black pepper, to taste

Directions:
1. Add everything in a food processor and pulse until a smooth mixture is formed. 2. Pour the mixture in Ninja Foodi cooking pot and select "Bake/Roast". 3. Close the Crisping Lid. 4. Bake for about 20 minutes at 205°C/400°F and open the lid. 5. Take out and serve hot.

Nutritional Values Per Serving: Calories: 95; Fat:6.9g; Carbs: 1.7g; Protein: 6.8g

Ninja Foodi Cinnamon Tea

Prep Time: 5 minutes
Cook Time: 12 minutes
Servings: 2
Ingredients:
240ml water
1 tsp black tea
2 cinnamon sticks
4 black peppercorns
120g fat-free cream
Directions:
1. Add water, peppercorns and cinnamon in the Ninja Foodi cooking pot. Close the Ninja Foodi with Pressure Lid and turn the pressure release valve to VENT position. Select the Ninja Foodi on Steam function. 2. Boil for about 10 minutes and add in cream. 3. Close the pressure lid and select "Pressure Cook" function. 4. Cook for about 2 minutes at LO. 5. Open the lid and strain the tea. 6. Serve hot and enjoy!
Nutritional Values Per Serving: Calories: 62; Fat: 0.8g; Carbs: 5.4g; Protein: 8.5g

Ninja Foodi Rocket Omelet

Prep Time: 10 minutes
Cook Time: 5 minutes
Servings: 4
Ingredients:
6 eggs

2 tbsp unsweetened almond milk
40g fresh rocket, chopped
4 spring onion, chopped finely
2 tbsp olive oil
Salt and black pepper, to taste
Directions:
1. Add everything except olive oil in a bowl. Whisk well. 2. Now, heat olive oil in the Cook & Crisp Basket of Ninja Foodi and add in egg mixture. 3. Select the "Steam" function and close the pressure Lid. Turn the pressure release valve to "VENT" position. 4. Cook for about 5 minutes. 5. Open the pressure lid and take out. 6. Serve and enjoy!
Nutritional Values Per Serving: Calories: 163; Fat: 13.8g; Carbs: 2.1g; Protein: 8.9g

Ninja Foodi Hard-boiled Eggs

Prep Time: 8-10 minutes
Cook Time: 15 minutes
Servings: 6
Ingredients:
12 eggs
240ml water
Ice cubes
Directions:
1. Place the multi-purpose pan filled with 240ml water inside Ninja Foodi. 2. Be very careful while placing the eggs in the Ninja Foodi. 3. Secure the pressure lid and turn the valve to Seal. Set the Ninja Foodi to High Pressure for 5 minutes. Press START/STOP. 4. While the eggs are being done, take a bowl, add ice cubes and water. 5. After 5 minutes, turn valve for Quick Pressure Release. Then take eggs out. 6. After taking out the eggs, put them in that ice bath for 5 minutes at least. 7. Peel and serve, the eggs are ready. They can also be stored in the fridge for up to a week!
Nutritional Values Per Serving: Calories: 155; Fat: 11g; Carbs: 1g; Protein: 6g

Spinach Turkey Cups

Prep Time: 15 minutes
Cook Time: 23 minutes
Servings: 4

Ingredients:
1 tbsp unsalted butter
450g fresh baby spinach
4 eggs
200g cooked turkey, chopped
4 tsp unsweetened almond milk
Black pepper and salt, as required

Directions:
1. Select the "Sauté/Sear" setting of Ninja Foodi at MD and place the butter into the cooking pot. 2. Heat the butter for about 2-3 minutes. 3. Add the spinach and cook for about 3 minutes or until just wilted. 4. Press the "Start/Stop" button to pause cooking and drain the liquid completely. 5. Transfer the spinach into a suitable bowl and set aside to cool slightly. 6. Set the Cook & Crisp Basket in the Ninja Foodi cooking pot. 7. Close the Ninja Foodi with Crisping Lid and select "Air Crisp." 8. Air Crisp at 180°C/355°F for 5 minutes. 9. Press the "Start/Stop" button to initiate preheating. 10. Divide the spinach into 4 greased ramekins, followed by the turkey. 11. Crack 1 egg into each ramekin and drizzle with almond milk. 12. Sprinkle with black pepper and salt. 13. After preheating, open the Ninja Foodi's lid. 14. Place the ramekins into the Cook &Crisp Basket. 15. Close the Ninja Foodi's lid with Crisping Lid and select "Air Crisp." 16. Set its cooking temperature to 180°C/355°F for 20 minutes. 17. Press the "Start/Stop" button to initiate cooking. 18. Open the Ninja Foodi's lid and serve hot.

Nutritional Values Per Serving: Calories: 200; Fat: 10.2g; Carbs: 4.5g; Protein: 23.4g

Vanilla Banana Bread

Prep Time: 10 minutes
Cook Time: 50 minutes
Servings: 8

Ingredients:
250gflour
1 tsp baking powder
100 g sweetener
115g butter softened
2 eggs
1 tbsp vanilla extract
4 bananas, peeled and mashed

Directions:
1. Grease a 18cm springform pan. 2. In a suitable bowl, mix flour and baking powder. 3. In another bowl, add sweetener, butter, and eggs and beat until creamy. 4. Add the bananas and vanilla extract and beat until well combined. 5. Slowly add flour mixture, 125g at a time, and mix until smooth. 6. Place the mixture into prepared loaf pan evenly. 7. In the Ninja Foodi cooking pot, place 240ml water. 8. Set the "Reversible Rack" in the Ninja Foodi cooking pot. 9. Place the pan over the "Reversible Rack." 10. Close the Ninja Foodi with the pressure lid and place the pressure valve to the "Seal" position. 11. Pressure cook the bread at HI for 50 minutes. 12. Switch the pressure valve to "Vent" and do a "Quick" release. 13. Cut into desired sized slices and serve.

Nutritional Values Per Serving: Calories: 336; Fat: 13.1 g; Carbs: 50.4 g; Protein: 5.4g

Avocado Cups

Prep Time: 10 minutes
Cook Time: 12 minutes
Servings: 2
Ingredients:
1 avocado, halved and pitted
Black pepper and salt, as required
2 eggs
1 tbsp Parmesan cheese, shredded
1 tsp fresh chives, minced
Directions:
1. Set a greased square piece of foil in Cook & Crisp Basket. 2. Set the Cook & Crisp Basket in the Ninja Foodi cooking pot. 3. Close the Ninja Foodi with Crisping Lid and select "Bake/Roast". 4. Set its cooking temperature to 200°C/390°F for 5 minutes. 5. Press the "Start/Stop" button to initiate preheating. 6. Carefully scoop out about 2 tsp of flesh from each avocado half. 7. Crack 1 egg in each avocado half and sprinkle with salt, black pepper, and cheese. 8. After preheating, open the lid. 9. Place the avocado halves into the Cook & Crisp Basket. 10. Close the Ninja Foodi with Crisping Lid and select "Bake/Roast." 11. Set its cooking temperature to 200°C/390°F for about 12 minutes. 12. Press the "Start/Stop" button to initiate cooking. 13. Open the Ninja Foodi's lid and transfer the avocado halves onto serving plates. 14. Top with Parmesan and chives and serve.
Nutritional Values Per Serving: Calories: 278; Fat: 24.7g; Carbs: 9.1g; Protein: 8.4g

Fruit Pancakes

Prep Time: 7 minutes
Cook Time: 20 minutes
Servings: 2
Ingredients:
65g pancake mix oats
2 eggs
60ml regular milk
1 tsp melted butter
2 drops vanilla essence
1 date
½ tsp cinnamon
120g any fresh fruit of your choice
Directions:
1. In a mixing bowl, mix together the pancake mix oats, eggs, melted butter, cinnamon, date, vanilla essence, and milk until a thick batter is prepared. 2. Gently mix in available fresh fruit, it can also be any thawed fruit. 3. Spray the Ninja Foodi cooking pot with spray oil. Non-sticky rapeseed spray could also be the best option. 4. Preheat your Ninja Foodi to 190°C/375°F on the Bake/Roast option. 5. After that, pour in the batter and it should be spread with even consistency throughout the Ninja Foodi. 6. Close the crisping lid of the Ninja Foodi and set the time of cooking to 12 to 15 minutes. 15 minutes are considered ideal for a perfect turnout of the pancake. 7. Lastly, serve it with any fruit or toppings of your choice.
Nutritional Values Per Serving: Calories: 227.5; Fat: 8.5g; Carbs: 18.5 g; Protein: 10.5 g

Egg Bites

Prep Time: 8 minutes
Cook Time: 12-15 minutes
Servings: 2
Ingredients:
3 egg whites
120g double cream
¼ tsp salt
35g chopped mushrooms
90g tomatoes
30g green onions
1 tbsp cheddar cheese
Water per requirement
Black pepper, as needed
Directions:
1. Take a container and whisk eggs, double cream, salt, and pepper together well. 2. Add up the remaining ingredients and again mix well. 3. Prepare the mold and spray with olive oil or use any greased baking tray. 4. Fill half of the mold with the mixture. Place its cover. 5. Place the Ninja Foodi Rack in the Low position. Put the covered mold onto the rack. In the Ninja Foodi cooking Pot, add 480ml water. Place covered mold on the rack. 6. Set the timer of the Steam option to 12 minutes. 7. Once ready, pop-out the egg bites of the mold!
Nutritional Values Per Serving: Calories: 140; Fat: 9.3g; Carbs: 2.5g; Protein: 3.8g

French Toast Bites

Prep Time: 10 minutes
Cook Time: 15 minutes
Servings: 1
Ingredients:
¼ loaf of French bread
2 eggs
2 tbsp milk
½ tsp cinnamon
1 mashed banana
Topping
1 tbsp brown sugar
1 tbsp honey
½ tsp cinnamon
Directions:
1. Cut the French bread into cubes and add it to a container. 2. In a separate small bowl, combine eggs, milk, mashed banana, honey, and cinnamon. 3. Pour mixture over the bread cubes and mix it all well till it's equally coated. 4. In a greased Ninja Foodi, add bread pieces in a single layer. 5. Sprinkle brown sugar and cinnamon on top of it. 6. Then select Air Crisp at 200°C/390°F for 10 minutes. Keep tossing or mixing halfway through. 7. When the golden-brown colour appears, drizzle the honey, bites are ready to be served!
Nutritional Values Per Serving: Calories: 302; Fat: 6g; Carbs: 21g; Protein: 13g

Swiss Bacon Frittata

Prep Time: 10 minutes
Cook Time: 30 minutes
Servings: 6
Ingredients:
1 small onion, chopped
225g raw bacon, chopped
450g frozen spinach
10 eggs
225g cottage cheese
120ml half cream
1 tsp salt
110g shredded Swiss cheese
Directions:
1. Set your Ninja Foodi at MD: HI on Sear/Sauté Mode. 2. Add bacon, and onion to the Ninja Foodi and sauté for 10 minutes until crispy. 3. Stir in spinach and stir cook for 3 minutes. 4. Whisk eggs with cottage cheese, salt, and half cream in a bowl. 5. Pour this mixture into the Ninja Foodi cooking pot. 6. Drizzle Swiss cheese over the egg mixture. 7. Secure the Ninja Foodi lid and switch the Foodi to Bake/Roast mode for 20 minutes at 175°C/350°F. 8. Serve warm.
Nutritional Values Per Serving: Calories 139; Total Fat 10.1g; Total Carbs 2.3g; Protein 10.1g

Breakfast Oats Bowl

Prep Time: 3 minutes
Cook Time: 8 minutes
Servings: 2
Ingredients:
80g oats
360ml milk
1.5 tsp ground cinnamon powder
Water as required
Optional Toppings:
Flax seeds
Honey
Granola mix
Directions:
1. Add all the ingredients in the Ninja Foodi. 2. Oats should be fully submerged in water. Secure the pressure lid and turn the valve to Seal. Set the Ninja Foodi to High Pressure for 5 minutes. 3. After 5 minutes turn the valve off and let the oats sit for about 5 minutes after being fully cooked and all pressure to release. 4. Serve with your favorite toppings!
Nutritional Values Per Serving: Calories: 162; Fat: 4.8g; Carbs: 12g; Protein: 9.3g

Courgette Egg Tots

Prep Time: 15 minutes
Cook Time: 9 minutes
Servings: 8
Ingredients:
2 medium courgettes
1 egg
1 tsp salt
½ tsp baking soda
1 tsp lemon juice
1 tsp basil
1 tbsp oregano
40g oat flour
1 tbsp olive oil
1 tsp minced garlic
1 tbsp butter
Directions:
1. Wash the courgette and grate it. Beat the egg in a suitable mixing bowl and blend it using a whisk. 2. Add the baking soda, lemon juice, basil, oregano, salt, and flour to the egg mixture. 3. Stir it carefully until smooth. Combine the grated courgette and egg mixture together. 4. Knead the dough until smooth. Mix olive oil with minced garlic together. 5. Set the Ninja Foodi's insert to "Sear/Sauté" mode. 6. Add butter and transfer the mixture to the Ninja Foodi's insert. Melt the mixture. 7. Make the small tots from the courgette dough and place them in the melted butter mixture. 8. Sauté the dish at MD for 3 minutes on each side. 9. Once the courgette tots are cooked, remove them from the Ninja Foodi's insert and serve.
Nutritional Values Per Serving: Calories: 64; Fat: 4.4g; Carbs: 4.35g; Protein: 2g

Herbed Cauliflower Fritters

Prep Time: 15 minutes
Cook Time: 13 minutes
Servings: 7
Ingredients:
450g cauliflower
1 medium white onion
1 tsp salt
½ tsp ground white pepper
1 tbsp sour cream
1 tsp turmeric
5g dill, chopped
1 tsp thyme
3 tbsp almond flour
1 egg
2 tbsp butter
Directions:
1. Wash the cauliflower and separate it into the florets. 2. Chop the florets and place them in a blender. 3. Peel the onion and dice it. Add the diced onion to a blender and blend the mixture. 4. When you get the smooth texture, add salt, ground white pepper, sour cream, turmeric, dill, thyme, and almond flour. 5. Add egg, blend the mixture well until a smooth dough form. 6. Remove the cauliflower dough from a blender and form into medium balls. 7. Flatten the balls a little. Set the Ninja Foodi's insert to "Sear/Sauté" mode. 8. Add the butter to the Ninja Foodi cooking pot and melt it. 9. Add the cauliflower fritters in the Ninja Foodi cooking pot, and sauté them for 6 minutes. 10. Flip them once. Cook the dish in "Sear/Sauté" mode for 7 minutes. 11. Once done, remove the fritters from the Ninja Foodi's insert. 12. Serve immediately.
Nutritional Values Per Serving: Calories: 143; Fat: 10.6g; Carbs: 9.9g; Protein: 5.6g

Garlicky Tomato

Prep Time: 10 minutes
Cook Time: 5 minutes
Servings: 5
Ingredients:
5 tomatoes
10g chives, chopped
50g garlic clove, minced
½ tsp salt
½ tsp black pepper
1 tbsp olive oil
200g Parmesan cheese
Directions:
1. Wash the tomatoes and slice them into thick slices. 2. Place the sliced tomatoes in the Ninja Foodi cooking pot. 3. Combine the grated cheese and minced garlic and stir the mixture. 4. Sprinkle the tomato slices with chives, black pepper, and salt. 5. Then sprinkle the sliced tomatoes with the cheese mixture. 6. Close the Ninja Foodi' cooking pot and cook the dish in the "Pressure" mode for 5 minutes at LO. 7. Once done, remove the tomatoes carefully and serve.
Nutritional Values Per Serving: Calories: 224; Fat: 14g; Carbs: 12.55g; Protein: 13g

Cashew Cream

Prep Time: 8 minutes
Cook Time: 10 minutes
Servings: 10
Ingredients:

350g cashew
500ml chicken stock
1 tsp salt
1 tbsp butter
2 tbsp ricotta cheese
Directions:
1. Combine the cashews with the chicken stock in the Ninja Foodi's insert. 2. Add salt and close the Ninja Foodi's lid. 3. Cook the dish in the "Pressure Cook" mode for 10 minutes at HI. 4. Remove the cashews from the Ninja Foodi's insert and drain the nuts from the water. 5. Transfer the cashews to a blender, and add the ricotta cheese and butter. 6. Blend the mixture until it is smooth. When you get the texture you want, remove it from a blender. 7. Serve it immediately, or keep the cashew butter in the refrigerator.
Nutritional Values Per Serving: Calories: 252; Fat: 20.6g; Carbs: 13.8g; Protein: 6.8g

Ninja Foodi Cheddar Biscuits

Prep Time: 10 minutes
Cook Time: 15 minutes
Servings: 8
Ingredients:
¼ tsp baking powder
70g butter
¼ tsp ginger powder
¼ tsp garlic powder
4 eggs
25g coconut flour, sifted
110g cheddar cheese
Salt, to taste
Directions:
1. Add flour, baking powder, garlic powder, ginger powder, and salt in a large bowl. Mix well. 2. Now, add butter and eggs in another bowl. Whisk well. 3. Combine the two mixtures and mix properly. Set aside. 4. Place the batter in Ninja Foodi. Close the unit with Crisping Lid and select the "Bake/Roast" function. 5. Bake for 15 minutes at 205°C/400°F and open the lid. 6. Take out, serve and enjoy!
Nutritional Values Per Serving: Calories: 155; Fat: 13g; Carbs: 3g; Protein: 6.9g

Ninja Foodi Spicy Peanuts

Prep Time: 5 minutes
Cook Time: 2 hours 40 minutes
Servings: 6
Ingredients:
200g peanuts
1½ tbsp chili seasoning mix
½ tbsp butter
Directions:
1. Add peanuts, chili seasoning mix, and butter in the pot of Ninja Foodi. Mix well. Close the unit with Pressure Lid and turn the pressure release valve to the VENT position. 2. Select "Slow Cook". 3. Cook for about 2 hours and 30 minutes at LO. Stir after every 30 minutes. 4. Open the lid and cook for 15 minutes. 5. Take out, serve and enjoy!
Nutritional Values Per Serving: Calories: 134; Fat: 11.1g; Carbs: 6.7g; Protein: 5.6g

Ninja Foodi Cod Sticks

Prep Time: 10 minutes
Cook Time: 15 minutes
Servings: 8
Ingredients:
100g almond flour
2 eggs
1 cod fillet, thinly sliced
2 tsp dried parsley, crushed

½ tsp cayenne pepper
Salt and black pepper, to taste
Directions:
1. Add eggs in one bowl and all the other ingredients except cod slices in another bowl. Mix well. 2. Dip cod slices first in egg mixture and then in the other mixture. Set aside. 3. Arrange cod slices in Ninja Foodi cooking pot. Close the unit with Crisping Lid and select to "Bake/Roast" function. 4. Bake for 6 minutes on each side at 175°C/350°F and open the lid. 5. Take out, serve and enjoy!
Nutritional Values Per Serving: Calories: 111; Fat: 7.9g; Carbs: 3.2g; Protein: 6.9g

Cheese Stuffed Dates

Prep Time: 5 minutes
Cook Time: 7 minutes
Serves: 7
Ingredients:
170g parmesan cheese, grated
230g ripe dates
1 tsp garlic, minced
1 tbsp sour cream
1 tsp butter
½ tsp ground white pepper
1 tsp oregano
Directions:
1. Remove the stones from the dates. 2. Combine the garlic, sour cream, ground white pepper, and oregano, and stir the mixture. Add in the parmesan. Blend the mixture until smooth. 3. Stuff the dates with the cheese mixture and place them on the lower position of the Reversible Rack. Then insert the rack in the Ninja Foodi's cooking pot. 4. Set the Ninja Foodi to Steam mode. 5. Add the butter and close the Pressure Lid. Cook for 7 minutes. 6. When the cooking time ends, remove the dates from the Ninja Foodi, let them rest briefly, and serve.
Nutritional Values Per Serving: Calories 203; Fat: 7.6g; Carbs: 28.3g; Protein: 8g

Ninja Foodi Spicy Popcorns

Prep Time: 10 minutes
Cook Time: 5 minutes
Servings: 6
Ingredients:
200g popping corns
2 tsp ground turmeric
½ tsp garlic powder
6 tbsp olive oil
Salt, to taste
Directions:
1. Heat 4 tbsp of olive-oil in the cooking pot and add popping corns in it. 2. Select "Sear/Sauté" and close the pressure Lid. Turn the pressure release valve in the VENT position. 3. Sauté for about 5 minutes at HI. 4. Take out and set aside. 5. Meanwhile, add remaining olive oil, turmeric, garlic powder, and salt in a bowl. Mix well. 6. Pour the mixture on popcorns and toss to coat well. 7. Serve and enjoy!
Nutritional Values Per Serving: Calories: 143; Fat: 14.1g; Carbs: 5.3g; Protein: 0.3g

Ninja Foodi Spinach Chips

Prep Time: 12 minutes
Cook Time: 10 minutes
Servings: 4
Ingredients:
½ tsp paprika

¼ tsp ground cumin
¼ tsp olive oil
60g fresh spinach leaves
Salt, to taste
Directions:
1. Add everything in a large bowl and mix well. Set aside. 2. Place spinach leaves in Ninja Foodi cooking pot. Close the unit with Crisping Lid and select to the "Bake/Roast" function. 3. Bake for about 10 minutes at 160°C/325°F and open the lid. 4. Take out, serve and enjoy!
Nutritional Values Per Serving: Calories: 7; Fat: 0.4g; Carbs: 0.7g; Protein: 0.5g

Avocado Deviled Eggs

Prep Time: 10 minutes
Cook Time: 5 minutes
Servings: 6
Ingredients:
6 eggs
1 avocado, peeled
1 tbsp cream
½ tsp minced garlic
240ml water for cooking
Directions:
1. Place the eggs in the Ninja Foodi's insert and add water. Close and seal the lid. 2. Cook the eggs on High-pressure mode for 5 minutes. 3. Then use natural pressure release for 5 minutes more. 4. After this, blend together avocado, minced garlic, and cream. 5. Once the mixture is smooth, transfer to the mixing bowl. 6. Peel the cooked eggs and cut them into halves. 7. Remove the eggs yolks and transfer them to the avocado mixture. 8. Fill the boiled egg whites with the avocado mixture. 9. Serve.
Nutritional Values Per Serving: Calories: 133; Fat: 11g; Carbs: 3.4g; Protein: 6.2g

Ninja Foodi Banana Cookies

Prep Time: 15 minutes
Cook Time: 20 minutes
Servings: 7
Ingredients:
1 banana, mashed
60ml soymilk
½ tbsp rapeseed oil
¼ tbsp baking powder
120g white flour
Directions:
1. Add mashed bananas, oil, and soymilk in a bowl. Mix well. 2. Add in flour and baking powder. Stir properly. 3. Knead the dough and roll it with the help of a rolling pin. 4. Cut the dough into circles and place them in Ninja Foodi. 5. Close the Crisping Lid and choose the "Bake/Roast" function. 6. Bake for about 20 minutes at 205°C/400°F. 7. Open the lid and take out. 8. Serve and enjoy!
Nutritional Values Per Serving: Calories: 94; Fat: 1.4g; Carbs: 18.3g; Protein: 2.3g

Nutmeg Peanuts

Prep Time: 5 minutes
Cook Time: 1.5 hour
Servings: 8
Ingredients:
750g peanuts in shells
1 tbsp salt
1L water
½ tsp nutmeg
Directions:

1. Combine the water, nutmeg, and salt together. 2. Stir the mixture well until salt is dissolved. 3. Transfer the water in the Ninja Foodi' cooking pot. 4. Add peanuts in shells and close the Ninja Foodi cooking pot. 5. Cook the dish on the "Pressure Cook" mode for 90 minutes at LO. 6. Once done, remove the peanuts from the Ninja Foodi's insert. 7. Let the peanuts cool before serving.
Nutritional Values Per Serving: Calories: 562; Fat: 36.8g; Carbs: 8.57g; Protein: 28g

Dried Tomatoes

Prep Time: 5 minutes
Cook Time: 8 hours
Servings: 8
Ingredients:
5 medium tomatoes
1 tbsp basil
1 tsp coriander, chopped
1 tbsp onion powder
5 tbsp olive oil
1 tsp paprika
Directions:
1. Wash the tomatoes and slice them. 2. Combine the coriander, basil, and paprika together and stir well. 3. Place the sliced tomatoes in the Ninja Foodi cooking pot and sprinkle them with the spice mixture. 4. Add olive oil and close the Ninja Foodi's pressure lid. Turn the pressure release valve to the VENT position. Cook the dish on the "Slow Cook" mode for 8 hours at LO. 5. Once done, the tomatoes should be semi-dry. 6. Remove them from the Ninja Foodi's insert. 7. Serve the dish warm or keep it in the refrigerator.
Nutritional Values Per Serving: Calories: 92; Fat: 8.6g; Carbs: 3.84g; Protein: 1g

Ninja Foodi Popcorn

Prep Time: 5 minutes
Cook Time: 10 minutes
Servings: 14

Ingredients:
3 tbsp oil, whatever kind you like
120g popcorn kernels
½ tsp salt
4 tbsp butter, salted and room temperature

Directions:
1. Measure out a piece of foil that is 10cm larger than the diameter of the Ninja Foodi cooking pot and wide enough to be able to fold into a pouch. Tuck the ends under the lip of the inner pot and make multiple holes with a thin sharp object. I used the pointy end of my cake tester. You don't want the holes too big or the butter will just pour out in places. 2. Add 3 tbsp of oil to the cooking pot and popped corn kernel. Cover the unit with Pressure Lid and turn the pressure release valve to VENT position. Turn the Ninja Foodi on HI Sear/Sauté function. 3. While you are waiting for the kernel to pop, cut or spread your butter on the foil. 4. When you hear the kernel pop, add in the remaining unpopped kernels and the salt. Stir to combine. 5. Close the foil packet and secure by tucking under the lid of the cooking pot. Cover with Pressure Lid. Leave the Sear/Sauté on HI until to begin to hear the kernels rapidly popping (less than one second between pops), turn the heat down to Medium/Low. Insert a spatula or wooden spoon and stir the bottom to move the kernels around. 6. Once the popping has slowed down to about one pop every few seconds, turn the Ninja Foodi off and stir again. If there is any butter left in the foil, shake it over the popcorn and stir. 7. Serve and enjoy!

Nutritional Values Per Serving: Calories: 78; Fat: 7g; Carbs: 4g; Protein: 1g

Pork Shank

Prep Time: 15 minutes
Cook Time: 45 minutes
Servings: 6

Ingredients:
450g pork shank
50g parsley, chopped
4 garlic cloves
1 tsp salt
½ tsp paprika
2 tbsp olive oil
1 tsp coriander, chopped
1 tbsp celery
1 carrot, grated
250ml water
1 red onion, chopped
80ml wine
2 tbsp lemon juice

Directions:
1. Chop the parsley and slice the garlic cloves. 2. Combine the vegetables together and add salt, paprika, coriander, wine, and lemon juice and stir the mixture. 3. Combine the pork shank and marinade together and leave the mixture. 4. Combine the sliced onion and grated carrot together. 5. Add celery and blend well. Add the vegetables together with olive oil to the pork shank mixture and stir using your hands. 6. Place the meat in the Ninja Foodi cooking pot and add water. 7. Close the Ninja Foodi's lid, and set the Ninja Foodi to "Pressure Cook" function. 8. Cook for 45 minutes at HI. Once done, remove the meat from the Ninja Foodi's insert and chill the dish well. 9. Slice the pork shank and serve.

Nutritional Values Per Serving: Calories: 242; Fat: 19.8g; Carbs: 5.38g; Protein: 11g

Ninja Foodi Spiced Almonds

Prep Time: 10 minutes
Cook Time: 14 minutes
Servings: 6
Ingredients:
2 tbsp unsweetened applesauce
160g almonds
¼ tsp cayenne pepper
¼ tsp ground cumin
½ tsp olive oil
½ tbsp water
¼ tsp ground cinnamon
¼ tsp red chili powder
Salt, to taste
Directions:
1. Arrange almonds in Ninja Foodi cooking pot and close the unit with Crisping Lid. Select the unit to "Bake/Roast" function. 2. Bake for about 10 minutes at 175°C/350°F and open the lid. 3. Take out and set aside. 4. Meanwhile, add oil, water and applesauce in a bowl. Mix well. 5. Add in almonds and toss to coat well. 6. Add cinnamon, ground cumin, red chili powder, cayenne pepper, and salt in another bowl. Mix well. 7. Arrange almonds again in the Ninja Foodi cooking pot and top them with cinnamon mixture. 8. Close the Crisping Lid. Set the unit on "Bake/Roast" function. 9. Bake them for about 4 minutes at 175°C/350°F and open the lid. 10. Take out, serve and enjoy!
Nutritional Values Per Serving: Calories: 98; Fat: 8.4g; Carbs: 4.2g; Protein: 3.4g

Courgette Muffins

Prep Time: 15 minutes
Cook Time: 15 minutes
Servings: 6
Ingredients:
60g coconut flour
1 medium courgette, finely chopped
1 tsp baking soda
1 tbsp lemon juice
½ tsp salt
½ tsp black pepper
1 tbsp butter
80ml coconut milk
1 tsp poppy seeds
2 tbsp flax meal
Directions:
1. Place the chopped courgette in a blender and mix until smooth. 2. Combine the salt, baking soda, lemon juice, poppy seeds, coconut flour, butter, black pepper, and flax meal together. 3. Add the milk and blended courgette. 4. Knead the dough until smooth. It can be a little bit sticky. 5. Place the muffins in the muffin's tins and transfer the courgette muffins in the Ninja Foodi's insert. 6. Cook the muffins on the "Steam" mode for 15 minutes. 7. Once done, check if the dish is done using a toothpick. 8. Once the muffins are cooked, remove them from the Ninja Foodi's insert and serve.
Nutritional Values Per Serving: Calories: 146; Fat: 8.9g; Carbs: 13.5g; Protein: 4g

Parmesan Breadsticks

Prep Time: 25 minutes
Cook Time: 10 minutes
Servings: 8

Ingredients:
1 tsp baking powder
½ tsp sweetener
½ tsp salt
250ml warm water
180g almond flour
125g Parmesan
1 tbsp olive oil
1 tsp onion powder
1 tsp basil

Directions:
1. Combine the baking powder, sweetener, and warm water in a mixing bowl. 2. Stir the mixture well. Add the almond flour, onion powder, salt, and basil. 3. Knead the dough until smooth. Separate dough into 10 pieces and make the long logs. 4. Twist the logs in braids. Grate the Parmesan cheese. 5. Place the twisted logs in the Ninja Foodi's insert. 6. Sprinkle the grated Parmesan cheese and olive oil, and close the Ninja Foodi with Pressure Lid. Turn the pressure release valve to SEAL position. 7. Cook the breadsticks at the "Pressure Cook" mode for 10 minutes at LO. 8. Release the pressure and remove the lid. 9. Leave the breadsticks for 10 minutes to rest. 10. Serve the breadsticks immediately or keep them in a sealed container.

Nutritional Values Per Serving: Calories: 242; Fat: 18.9g; Carbs: 2.7g; Protein: 11.7g

Breadsticks

Prep Time: 25 minutes
Cook Time: 10 minutes
Serves: 8

Ingredients:
1 tsp baking powder
½ tsp sweetener
½ tsp salt
240ml warm water
250 g almond flour
140g parmesan, grated
1 tbsp olive oil
1 tsp onion powder
1 tsp basil

Directions:
1. Combine the baking powder, sweetener, and warm water in a mixing bowl. 2. Stir the mixture well. Add the almond flour, onion powder, salt, and basil. 3. Knead the dough until smooth. 4. Separate the dough into 10 pieces to make long logs. Twist the logs into braids. 5. Preheat the Ninja Foodi on Bake/Roast mode for 10 minutes at 160°C/325°F. 6. Place the twisted logs into the cooking pot of the Ninja Foodi. 7. Sprinkle the logs with the grated parmesan cheese and the olive oil, and close the lid. 8. Bake the breadsticks on Bake/Roast mode for 15 minutes at 160°C/325°F. 9. Leave the breadsticks for 10 minutes to rest.

Nutritional Values Per Serving: Calories 242; Fat: 18.9g; Carbs: 2.7g; Protein: 11.7g

Ninja Foodi Spicy Cashews

Prep Time: 10 minutes
Cook Time: 2 hours 45 minutes
Servings: 12

Ingredients:
375g cashews
3 tbsp chili seasoning mix
1½ tbsp butter

Directions:
1. Add everything in the pot of Ninja Foodi and mix well. 2. Close the Pressure Lid. Turn the pressure release valve to VENT position and select "Slow Cook". 3. Cook for about 2 hours and 30 minutes on LO. 4. Open the lid and cook for 15 more minutes. 5. Take out, serve and enjoy!

Serving Suggestions: Top with red chili powder before serving.

Variation Tip: You can add cayenne pepper for a stronger taste.

Nutritional Values Per Serving: Calories: 741; Fat: 61.2g; Carbs: 40.2g; Protein: 18.6g

Japanese Eggs

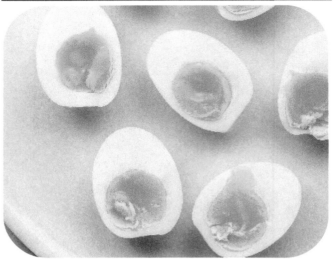

Prep Time: 30 minutes
Cook Time: 20 minutes
Servings: 4

Ingredients:
240ml Chinese master stock
4 eggs
1 tsp salt

Directions:
1. Pour the Chinese master stock in the Ninja Foodi's insert and close the Ninja Foodi's pressure lid. 2. Cook the liquid on the "Pressure" mode for 10 minutes at LO. 3. Remove the Chinese master stock from the Ninja Foodi's insert and chill it. 4. Meanwhile, place the eggs in the Ninja Foodi's insert. 5. Add water and boil the eggs on the "Pressure" mode at LO for 10 minutes. 6. Once eggs are done, remove from the Ninja Foodi's insert and chill well. 7. Peel the eggs and place them in the Chinese master stock. 8. Leave the eggs in the liquid for 20 minutes. 9. Remove the eggs from the liquid. Cut the eggs into halves.

Nutritional Values Per Serving: Calories: 134; Fat: 9.7g; Carbs: 2.01g; Protein: 9g

Chicken Potato Stew

Prep Time: 10-15 minutes
Cook Time: 8-10 minutes
Servings: 4-6
Ingredients:
900g boneless chicken thighs
4 potatoes (coarsely sliced)
Salt and pepper to taste
2-3 peppercorns
2 tbsp olive oil
1 tbsp thyme
½ tbsp onion powder
1 tsp paprika powder
1 tbsp chopped garlic
4 tbsp chopped onion
120ml chicken stock
Directions:
1. Start by combining thyme, paprika, salt, pepper, and onion powder. Now take chicken thighs and season both sides with this spice mix. 2. Put olive oil in Ninja Foodi and select the Air Crisp Mode at 200°C/390°F. 3. Air Crisp chicken thigh cuts in Ninja Foodi. Cook each side for about 2 to 3 minutes. Now take out the chicken and set it aside. 4. Add onions and chopped garlic to the Ninja Foodi. Add the peppercorns and steam for about 2 minutes. Now add chicken stock to it and continue to cook. 5. Now add potatoes and chicken, select Pressure Cook, and cook on Pressure Cook setting at HI for 8 minutes. Then allow it to naturally release for about four to 5 minutes then quick release!
Nutritional Values Per Serving: Calories: 385; Fat: 16.3g; Carbs: 7.7g; Protein: 35.5g

Mexican Chicken with Rice

Prep Time: 12-15 minutes
Cook Time: 10 minutes
Servings: 4
Ingredients:
450g chicken breasts, boneless
185g uncooked rice
Salt to taste
½ tsp chili flakes
2-3 minced garlic cloves
255g black beans
40g corn
120ml chicken stock
25g cheese
2 diced onion
1 tbsp olive oil
Directions:
1. Turn on the Ninja Foodi on Pressure Cook mode at 200°C/390°F and then add olive oil. 2. Add onions, garlic powder, chicken cubes, chili flakes, and salt once oil is hot and cook it until the protein changes its colour. 3. Dump in black beans and corn alongside chicken stock after turning off the Ninja Foodi. Stir well together. 4. Now on top of that, sprinkle uncooked rice and by using the back of the spoon, submerge it into the liquid but don't stir it. 5. Put the lid back on and close the steam valve for 9 minutes. After that let it naturally release pressure. 6. Lift the lid, fluff up the rice mixture and add cheese on top, mix it gently and set the top back again for about 3 minutes for the cheese to melt!
Nutritional Values Per Serving: Calories: 31.5; Fat: 14.4g; Carbs: 31.5g; Protein: 61g

Bagel Chicken Tenders

Prep Time: 8 minutes
Cook Time: 15-20 minutes
Servings: 2
Ingredients:
6-8 chicken tenders
55g bread crumbs
2 tbsp bagel seasoning
1 egg
Directions:
1. Start by washing the chicken breasts and cut them into tenders. You can also buy chicken tenderloins. 2. Now take two bowls and add egg to one and bread crumb mixture to the other. Add bagel seasoning to the bread crumbs and mix it well. 3. Prepare one tender at a time by first coating it with an egg then rolling it in the crumb mixture. 4. Air Crisp it in the Ninja Foodi by selecting Air Crisp Mode at 200°C/390°F for 20 minutes in a single layer.
Nutritional Values Per Serving: Calories: 433; Fat: 6.3g; Carbs: 15.9g; Protein: 44.3g

Glazed Chicken & Vegetables

Prep Time: 8-10 minutes
Cook Time: 20-25 minutes
Servings: 2
Ingredients:
225g chicken thighs boneless
2 tbsp soya sauce
2 tsp Worcestershire sauce
2 tbsp brown sugar
4 crushed garlic cloves
450g bag of frozen mixed vegetables
1 tbsp vinegar optional
1 tbsp olive oil
Black pepper to taste
Directions:
1. Start by adding soya sauce, Worcestershire sauce, brown sugar, and garlic in a closable container or zip lock bag. Now add chicken in it and seal to coat it well with the marinade. Let it rest in the fridge for 2 to 3 hours. 2. Oil spray the Cook & Crisp Basket. Now put vegetables and chicken in the Cook & Crisp Basket. 3. Give a spray of olive oil again and sprinkle just a pinch of salt if preferred. 4. Air Crisp it for about 25 minutes at 200°C/390°F. 5. When the chicken reaches 75°C internally, serve it!
Nutritional Values Per Serving: Calories: 397; Fat: 11.3g; Carbs: 25.5g; Protein: 27.4g

Ninja Foodi Chicken & Carrot Stew

Prep Time: 10 minutes
Cook Time: 6 hours
Servings: 3
Ingredients:
2 (110g) boneless chicken breasts, cubed
50g chopped onions
½ tsp dried thyme
1 garlic clove, minced
190g cubed carrots
90g chopped tomatoes
240ml chicken stock
Salt and black pepper, to taste
Directions:
1. Add everything in the Ninja Foodi and select "Slow Cook". 2. Close the pressure Lid. 3. Cook for about 6 hours at HI and take out. 4. Serve and enjoy!
Nutritional Values Per Serving: Calories: 226; Fat: 6.4g; Carbs: 16.6g; Protein: 25g

Ninja Foodi Basil Pesto Chicken

Prep Time: 20 minutes
Cook Time: 30 minutes
Servings: 4
Ingredients:
4 boneless chicken breasts
3 garlic cloves, minced
70g pine nuts
50g fresh basil leaves
½ tsp red pepper flakes
120ml olive oil
Salt and black pepper, to taste
Directions:
1. Add olive oil, garlic, pine nuts, basil, and red pepper flakes in a food processor. Pulse well. 2. Now, arrange chicken breasts in the pot of Ninja Foodi and pour basil mixture on it. 3. Close the Crisping Lid and select "Bake/Roast" mode. 4. Bake for about 30 minutes at 190°C/375°F. 5. Open the Crisping Lid and take out. 6. Serve and enjoy!
Nutritional Values Per Serving: Calories: 603; Fat: 47.3g; Carbs: 3.4g; Protein: 43.4g

Ninja Foodi Duck Fajita Platter

Prep Time: 10 minutes
Cook Time: 25 minutes
Servings: 4
Ingredients:
450g duck breasts, sliced
½ green sweet pepper, chopped
½ red sweet pepper, chopped
1 onion, sliced
2 tbsp olive oil
1 tsp garlic powder
1 tsp ground cumin
2 tsp chili powder
½ tsp dried oregano
Salt, to taste
Directions:
1. Add duck breasts, green sweet pepper, red sweet pepper, and garlic powder in a large bowl. Mix well. 2. Add in chili powder, cumin, onion, olive oil, oregano and salt in the bowl. Toss to coat well. 3. Place the duck breasts in the pot of Ninja Foodi. Close the unit with Crisping Lid and select "Bake/Roast" function. 4. Bake for about 25 minutes at 205°C/400°F and open the lid. 5. Take out and serve hot.
Nutritional Values Per Serving: Calories: 237; Fat: 12g; Carbs: 6.7g; Protein: 26.1g

Ninja Foodi Chicken Stock

Prep Time: 10 minutes
Cook Time: 3 hours
Servings: 3
Ingredients:
675g chicken
1 bay leaf
1 celery stalk, chopped
¼ tsp dried rosemary, crushed
1 carrot, chopped
¼ tsp dried thyme
4 peppercorns
1 onion, quartered
960ml cold water
Directions:
1. Add everything in a Ninja Foodi and select "Slow Cook". 2. Simmer at HI for about 3 hours and open the lid. 3. Take out and set aside. 4. Strain the stock and serve hot.
Nutritional Values Per Serving: Calories: 1281; Fat: 25.3g; Carbs: 5.9g; Protein: 241.6g

Chicken Pasta with Dried Tomatoes

Prep Time: 6 minutes
Cook Time: 15-20 minutes
Servings: 4
Ingredients:
450g chicken thigh
500g penne pasta
1 tbsp butter
1 diced onion
1 tsp chopped garlic
30g dried tomatoes
1 tbsp tomato paste
1 tbsp Italian Seasoning
Salt to taste
2 tbsp parmesan cheese
60g double cream
2 tbsp cream cheese
60ml chicken stock
1 tbsp extra-virgin olive oil
Directions:
1. When water comes to a boil, boil the pasta, don't forget to add salt to the pasta water. You can simply boil according to the given instructions on the package. 2. On the other hand, cut the chicken into strips. Preheat the Ninja Foodi on Low Pressure setting. 3. Add half the oil and butter into a large frying pan. Let it melt. 4. Add chicken and let it cook for 3 to 4 minutes. 5. Flip and cook it for another 2 minutes. Now take out the chicken from the pan. 6. Keep Ninja Foodi to Low Pressure Mode. Now add the remaining olive oil and onion into the pan and cook the onions until they become translucent. 7. Add garlic and cook it for about 1 minute. Then add tomato paste and dried tomatoes. 8. Season it with salt and Italian seasoning and mix it well. 9. Now add chicken stock and let it simmer for 2 minutes. 10. Add parmesan cheese, double cream, cream cheese, and stir it well. After the cheese melts, add chicken into it, then pour it over the pasta, and serve it hot!

Nutritional Values Per Serving: Calories: 470; Fat: 14.5g; Carbs: 59g; Protein: 24.8g

Ninja Foodi Turkey & Beans Wrap

Prep Time: 10 minutes
Cook Time: 13 minutes
Servings: 3
Ingredients:
110g lean turkey mince
¼ tsp ground cumin
3 cos lettuce leaves
¼ tsp garlic powder
1½ tbsp tomato sauce
65g cooked black beans
25g chopped onion
1½ tbsp extra-virgin olive oil
Salt and black pepper, to taste
Directions:
1. Add turkey, onion, tomato sauce, garlic powder, cumin, salt and pepper in a large bowl. Mix well. 2. Meanwhile, heat oil in a Ninja Foodi and add turkey mixture in it. 3. Select "Pressure Cook" mode. 4. Cook at LO for 10 minutes and then stir in tomato sauce and beans. 5. Cook for about 3 minutes and take out. 6. Divide the mixture evenly on lettuce leaves and serve.

Nutritional Values Per Serving: Calories: 356; Fat: 28.7g; Carbs: 14.8g; Protein: 12.5g

Chicken Vegetable Soup

Prep Time: 8 minutes
Cook Time: 3 minutes
Servings: 2
Ingredients:
225g boneless chicken thigh (bite-size cuts)
1 diced carrot
1 chopped onion
1 tsp garlic
55g boiled pasta
960ml stock
1 tsp salt
¾ tsp white pepper
1 tbsp soy sauce
1 tsp oregano
¼ tsp red chili powder
2 bay leaves
60g corn flour slurry
Directions:
1. In the Ninja Foodi, add carrots, onion, garlic, bay leaves then add the bite-size chicken cuts. 2. Now season it with salt, white pepper, oregano, red chili powder, and soy sauce and pour in the chicken stock. 3. Give it a good stir. Now set the valve to Seal and install the Pressure Lid. 4. Select the Pressure Cook function and set it to HI. Cook for 2 minutes. Usually, the pressure takes about 10 minutes to start building up. 5. Once it beeps, allow the pressure to naturally release for about 10 minutes after the completion of pressure cooking. And quickly release any remaining pressure by setting the valve to venting. 6. Now take out the bay leaves and discard them, select the option Steam and, let the soup simmer for another 3 to 5 minutes. 7. Pour in slurry and stir it well. Give it a boil until it's completely thickened. Serve instantly!
Nutritional Values Per Serving: Calories: 389; Fat: 10.3g; Carbs: 16g; Protein: 31.9g

Chicken Saltimbocca

Prep Time: 6 minutes
Cook Time: 10-15 minutes
Servings: 2
Ingredients:
2 chicken cutlets
2 tbsp plain flour
2-3 slices dry ham/prosciutto
2-3 sage leaves large
Pepper as required
1 tbsp extra-virgin olive oil
1 tbsp butter
Directions:
1. Put the flour in a shallow dish. Fold each chicken cutlet in the flour and coat evenly. Make sure to shake off the excess flour. Now arrange the cutlets on a plate, place a slice of prosciutto on it and add a sage leaf over it and then secure it with a toothpick. 2. Take extra-virgin olive oil in Steam Mode in Ninja Foodi. 3. Align chicken cutlets in a single layer in the pot and make sure the prosciutto side is down. 4. Sear the chicken from one side until it's golden and crispy then flip the cutlets and season it with pepper. Until the chicken is cooked, continue to sear. 5. Take out the chicken from the pot, arrange it on the platter and cover it with foil to keep it warm. Now add the butter to the pot and cook it until it starts foaming. 6. Pour wine to it and gently stir it to combine. Now pour the sauce onto the chicken cutlets and it's ready to be served immediately!
Nutritional Values Per Serving: Calories: 319; Fat: 18.1g; Carbs: 12g; Protein: 28g

Honey Garlic Chicken

Prep Time: 12 minutes
Cook Time: 15-20 minutes
Servings: 2
Ingredients:
450g bone-in chicken pieces
1 tbsp sesame oil
60ml stock
2 tbsp honey
2 tbsp soy sauce
½ tbsp apple cider vinegar
1 tsp chopped garlic
Salt to taste
Pepper to taste
1 tbsp corn flour
60ml water
Directions:
1. Combine honey, stock, soy sauce, and apple cider vinegar in a bowl and whisk it well. 2. Meanwhile, add chicken and garlic to the Ninja Foodi. Steam for 2 to 3 minutes and pour the chicken stock mixture. 3. Now Seal the pressure lid and secure the valve and set Ninja Foodi on Pressure Cook at High and cook for 8 minutes. 4. Whisk corn flour water together in a small bowl and prepare a slurry while the chicken is being cooked. 5. After 8 minutes, allow natural release of pressure for about 10 minutes and then turn it to quick release manually. Carefully open the lid and take it out then set Ninja Foodi on Pressure Cook at LO and mix the slurry into the sauce and keep stirring. Allow it to thicken for about 2 to 3 minutes. Coat all the chicken well. 6. Garnish it with some fresh green onion and a few sesame seeds!
Nutritional Values Per Serving: Calories: 219; Fat: 13.4g; Carbs: 11.7g; Protein: 22.8g

Jalapeno Chicken Nachos

Prep Time: 8-9 minutes
Cook Time: 8-9 minutes
Servings: 2
Ingredients:
30g tortillas chips
450g minced chicken
60g BBQ sauce
Salt to taste
120ml chicken stock
55g cheddar cheese
½ corn
2 tbsp chopped olives
50g sliced jalapeno
1 coarsely cut onion
Coriander to garnish
Directions:
1. Add the chicken, stock, and salt to a Ninja Foodi. For 8 minutes, Pressure Cook it on HI and releases the pressure when finished quickly. 2. Stir in BBQ sauce after draining the liquid. 3. At 200°C/390°F, preheat the Ninja Foodi at Air Crisp Mode. Take Cook & Crisp Basket and align the parchment paper. 4. Place tortilla chips on the base. Now give a layer of shredder BBQ chicken and corn and top it off with cheddar cheese evenly. 5. For about 5 to 10 minutes, place it in the Ninja Foodi and wait until cheese is melted. Then add olives, onions, and jalapenos slice to the desired amount. Follow it by adding fresh coriander!
Nutritional Values Per Serving: Calories: 550; Fat: 25.5g; Carbs: 29.7g; Protein: 55g

Ninja Foodi Chicken & Salsa Chili

Prep Time: 10 minutes
Cook Time: 8 hours 5 minutes
Servings: 4
Ingredients:
300g salsa
180ml water
½ jalapeno pepper, minced
½ tsp ground cumin
1 tsp chili powder
225g boneless chicken breast
1 garlic clove, minced
½ onion, chopped
½ avocado, chopped
1½ green sweet peppers, chopped
Salt and black pepper, to taste
Directions:
1. Add chicken, garlic, cumin, salsa, and water in a Ninja Foodi. Close the unit with Pressure Lid and turn the pressure release valve to VENT position. Select "Slow Cook". 2. Cook for about 6 hours on HI and open the lid. 3. Meanwhile, heat the non-stick frying pan and cook onions, jalapeno pepper, and sweet pepper in it for about 5 minutes. 4. Now, take the chicken out of the Ninja Foodi and shred it properly. 5. Place it back in the Slow Cook along with onion mixture, chili powder, avocado, salt, and pepper. Mix well. 6. Cook for about 2 hours and take out. 7. Serve and enjoy!
Nutritional Values Per Serving: Calories: 239; Fat: 9.8g; Carbs: 20.7g; Protein: 19.9g

Ninja Foodi Spinach Chicken

Prep Time: 10 minutes
Cook Time: 10 minutes
Servings: 4
Ingredients:
450g chicken mini-fillets
2 tbsp sour cream
2 garlic cloves, minced
100g chopped spinach
2 tbsp olive oil
20g parmesan cheese, shredded
Salt and black pepper, to taste
Directions:
1. Heat half of the olive oil in a Ninja Foodi and add chicken, salt, and pepper in it. 2. Select "Pressure Cook". 3. Cook for about 2 minutes per side at HI and take out the chicken. Set aside. 4. Add remaining oil in the pot of Ninja Foodi and sauté garlic in it for about 1 minute. 5. Add spinach, cream, and cheese in the frying pan and cook for about 2 minutes. 6. Place chicken in the Ninja Foodi cooking pot and simmer for about 5 minutes. 7. Take out and serve hot.
Serving Suggestions: Serve with onion rings on the top.
Variation Tip: Mozzarella cheese can also be used.
Nutritional Values Per Serving: Calories: 301; Fat: 17.1g; Carbs: 1.6g; Protein: 34.3g

Pulled Barbecue Chicken

Prep Time: 6 minutes
Cook Time: 9-10 minutes
Servings: 2
Ingredients:
450g chicken breast
240ml stock
4 tbsp BBQ sauce
½ tsp liquid smoke
Salt and pepper to taste
Directions:
1. Now inside the Ninja Foodi, place the chicken breast and sprinkle a little salt and pepper on both sides. 2. Then, add in stock over the chicken breasts, and install the Pressure Lid and switch the vent knob to Seal properly. Select the High option of the Cook on Pressure setting function for about 8 minutes. 3. Quickly release the pressure on food after the timer goes off and then remove the lid carefully. 4. Make sure that stock is reduced to half. Then add the barbecue sauce and let it cook on Air Crisp Mode at 200°C/390°F for 5 to 10 minutes. Make sure to shred it a bit with a spatula or fork. 5. Add the liquid smoke and it's good to go!
Nutritional Values Per Serving: Calories: 311; Fat: 4g; Carbs: 6.1g; Protein: 34.7g

Ninja Foodi Barbeque Chicken Drumsticks

Prep Time: 10 minutes
Cook Time: 8 hours
Servings: 4
Ingredients:
12 chicken drumsticks
2 tbsp red chili powder
1 tsp onion powder
1 tsp garlic powder
4 tbsp honey
2 tbsp apple cider vinegar
240g barbeque sauce
1 tbsp paprika
½ tbsp ground cumin
Salt and black pepper, to taste
Directions:
1. Add everything except honey in a Ninja Foodi. Close the unit with Pressure Lid, turn the pressure release valve to VENT position. Select "Slow Cook". 2. Cook for about 8 hours at HI and open the lid. 3. Take out the drumsticks and pour honey on them. 4. Serve and enjoy!
Nutritional Values Per Serving: Calories: 416; Fat: 9.1g; Carbs: 44.4g; Protein: 39g

Ninja Foodi Duck Stock

Prep Time: 10 minutes
Cook Time: 8 hours
Servings: 16
Ingredients:
1 roasted duck, meat removed
2 tsp apple cider vinegar
1.9 L water
2 carrots, chopped
2 onions, chopped
Salt, to taste
Directions:
1. Add duck bones in the Ninja Foodi and sprinkle some salt on it. 2. Add in remaining ingredients. Close the unit with Pressure Lid and turn the pressure release valve to VENT position. Select "Slow Cook". 3. Cook for 8 hours at LO and open the lid. 4. Take out the stock and serve.
Nutritional Values Per Serving: Calories: 21; Fat: 0.7g; Carbs: 2g; Protein: 1.8g

Pineapple Chicken

Prep Time: 2 hours
Cook Time: 9-10 minutes
Servings: 2
Ingredients:
2 chicken steaks
1 tbsp onion paste
4 tbsp teriyaki sauce
2 tbsp pineapple juice
1 tbsp ginger garlic paste
Salt and pepper to taste
Coriander and coriander to garnish
Directions:
1. Take a large bowl and combine all ingredients. Refrigerate it overnight. 2. Now remove it from the refrigerator and place the leftover marination in the bowl. 3. Place the chicken steak directly in the Ninja Foodi. 4. Now over Ninja Foodi on Pressure Cook mode at HI, cook the chicken for 3 minutes and use the reserved marinade to baste when meat is cooked halfway. 5. Now turn over the meat for 5 to 7 minutes to cook and do this until the meat is cooked properly. 6. Turn off and plate the chicken, and garnish it with fresh coriander or coriander!
Nutritional Values Per Serving: Calories: 391; Fat: 18.1g; Carbs: 36.4g; Protein: 20.4g

Pork Meatballs

Prep Time: 30 minutes
Cook Time: 6 minutes
Servings: 4
Ingredients:
450g pork mince
60g double cream
2 tsp salt
½ tsp ground caraway seeds
1½ tsp black pepper
¼ tsp ground allspice
2 courgettes, shredded
120ml almond milk
2 tbsp unsalted butter
Directions:
1. Transfer meat to a suitable bowl and add cream, 1 tsp salt, caraway seeds, ½ tsp pepper, and allspice, and mix it well. 2. Let the mixture chill for 30 minutes. 3. Once the mixture is ready, use your hands to scoop the mixture into meatballs. 4. Add half of your balls to the Ninja Foodi pot and cover with half of the courgettes. 5. Add remaining balls and cover with rest of the cabbage. 6. Add milk, pats of butter, season with black pepper and salt. 7. Lock and secure the Ninja Foodi's lid, then cook on "HIGH" pressure for 4 minutes. 8. Quick-release pressure. 9. Unlock and secure the Ninja Foodi's lid and serve. 10. Enjoy.
Nutritional Values Per Serving: Calories: 294; Fat: 26g; Carbs: 4g; Protein: 12g

Eastern Lamb Stew

Prep Time: 1 hour and 30 minutes
Cook Time: 60 minutes
Servings: 4
Ingredients:
2 tbsp olive oil
675g lamb stew meat, sliced into cubes
1 onion, diced
6 garlic cloves, chopped
1 tsp cumin
1 tsp coriander
1 tsp turmeric
1 tsp cinnamon
Black pepper and salt to taste
2 tbsp tomato paste
60ml red wine vinegar
2 tbsp maple syrup
300ml chicken stock
375g chickpeas, rinsed and drained
Directions:
1. Choose Sear/Sauté function in the Ninja Foodi. Stir in the oil. Sauté onion at MD for 3 minutes. 2. Add the lamb and seasonings. Cook for 5 minutes, stirring frequently. 3. Stir in the rest of the ingredients. Cover the pot. Set it to Pressure Cook. 4. Cook at "HI" pressure for 50 minutes. Release the pressure naturally. 5. Serve with quinoa. 6. Freeze and serve the next day for a more intense flavour.
Nutritional Values Per Serving: Calories: 867; Fat: 26.6g; Carbs: 87.4g; Protein: 71.2g

Beef Jerky

Prep Time: 10 minutes
Cook Time: 20 minutes
Servings: 4
Ingredients:
225g beef, sliced into ¼cm-thick strips
120ml soy sauce
2 tbsp Worcestershire sauce
2 tsp black pepper
1 tsp onion powder
½ tsp garlic powder
1 tsp salt
Directions:
1. Add listed ingredient to a large-sized ziploc bag, seal it shut. 2. Shake well, seal and leave it in the fridge overnight. 3. Lay strips on the deluxe reversible rack in the pot in the lower position, making sure not to overlap them. 4. Lock Crisping Lid and set its cooking temperature to 60°C/135°F, cook for 7 hours.
Nutritional Values Per Serving: Calories: 62; Fat: 7g; Carbs: 2g; Protein: 9g

Maple Glazed Pork Chops

Prep Time: 45 minutes
Cook Time: 12 minutes
Servings: 4
Ingredients:
2 tbsp maple syrup
4 tbsp mustard
2 tbsp garlic, minced
Black pepper and salt to taste
4 pork chops
Cooking spray
Directions:
1. Mix the maple syrup, mustard, garlic, black pepper, and salt in a suitable bowl. 2. Marinate the pork chops in the mixture for 20 minutes. 3. Place the pork chops on the Ninja Foodi basket. 4. Put the basket inside the pot. Seal with the Crisping Lid. 5. Set it to Air Crisp. Cook at 175°C/350°F for about 12 minutes, flipping halfway through.
Nutritional Values Per Serving: Calories: 348; Fat: 23.3g; Carbs: 14g; Protein: 21.1g

Braised Lamb Shanks

Prep Time: 20 minutes
Cook Time: 46 minutes
Servings: 4
Ingredients:
2 tbsp olive oil
4 lamb shanks
Black pepper and salt to taste
4 cloves garlic, minced
180ml dry red wine
1 tsp dried basil
¾ tsp dried oregano
800g crushed tomatoes
Directions:
1. Turn the Ninja Foodi to Sear/Sauté. Stir in the oil. Season the lamb with black pepper and salt. 2. Cook until brown. Remove and set aside. Add the garlic and cook for 15 seconds. 3. Pour in the wine. Simmer for 2 minutes. Stir in the basil, oregano, and tomatoes. 4. Put the lamb back to the pot. Seal the pot. Set it to Pressure Cook. 5. Cook at "HI" pressure for 45 minutes. Release the pressure naturally. 6. Serve over polenta.
Nutritional Values Per Serving: Calories: 790; Fat: 31g; Carbs: 18.3g; Protein: 96.8g

Bacon Strips

Prep Time: 5 minutes
Cook Time: 7 minutes
Servings: 2
Ingredients:
10 bacon strips
¼ tsp chilli flakes
⅓ tsp salt
¼ tsp basil, dried
Directions:
1. Rub the bacon strips with chilli flakes, dried basil, and salt. 2. Turn on your air fryer and place the bacon on the rack. 3. Lock the unit with the Crisping Lid. Select the unit on Bake/Roast function and then cook the bacon at 205°C/400°F for 5 minutes. 4. Cook for 3 minutes more if the bacon is not fully cooked. Serve and enjoy.
Nutritional Values Per Serving: Calories: 500; Fat: 46g; Carbs: 0g; Protein: 21g

Corned Cabbage Beef

Prep Time: 10 minutes
Cook Time: 100 minutes
Servings: 4
Ingredients:
1 corned beef brisket
960ml water
1 small onion, peeled and quartered
3 garlic cloves, smashed and peeled

2 bay leaves
3 whole black peppercorns
½ tsp allspice berries
1 tsp dried thyme
5 medium carrots
1 cabbage, cut into wedges
Directions:
1. Stir in corned beef, onion, garlic cloves, water, allspice, peppercorn, thymes to the Ninja Foodi. 2. Lock up the lid and cook for about 90 minutes at "HI" pressure. 3. Allow the pressure to release naturally once done. 4. Open up and transfer the meat to your serving plate. 5. Cover it with tin foil and allow it to cool for 15 minutes. 6. Stir in carrots and cabbage to the lid and let them cook for 10 minutes at "HI" pressure. 7. Once done, do a quick release. Take out the prepped veggies and serve with your corned beef.
Nutritional Values Per Serving: Calories: 297; Fats: 17g; Carbs:1g; Protein: 14g

Ninja Foodi Pork Shoulder Roast

Prep Time: 10 minutes
Cook Time: 10 hours
Servings: 14
Ingredients:
960g pork shoulder roast
4 carrots, peeled and sliced
4 onions, sliced
4 tbsp Italian seasonings
Salt and black pepper, to taste
Directions:
1. Add pork shoulder, Italian seasonings, salt, and pepper in a large bowl. Mix well and set aside for about 4 hours. 2. Now, place carrots and onions in the bottom of Ninja Foodi and add marinated pork shoulder in it. Close the unit with Pressure Lid and turn the pressure release valve to VENT position. 3. Select "Slow Cook". 4. Cook for about 10 hours on LO. 5. Open the pressure Lid and take out. 6. Serve and enjoy!
Nutritional Values Per Serving: Calories: 365; Fat: 27.6g; Carbs: 5.1g; Protein: 22.3g

Adobo Steak

Prep Time: 5 minutes
Cook Time: 25 minutes
Servings: 4
Ingredients:
480ml water
8 steaks, cubed, 800g pack
Pepper to taste
1¾ tsp adobo seasoning
1 can (200g) tomato sauce
45g green pitted olives
2 tbsp brine
1 small red pepper
½ medium onion, sliced
Directions:
1. Chop peppers and onions into ½cm strips. 2. Prepare beef by seasoning with adobo and pepper. 3. Add into Ninja Foodi cooking pot. 4. Stir in remaining ingredients and lock lid, cook on "HI" pressure for 25 minutes. 5. Release pressure naturally. 6. Serve and enjoy.
Nutritional Values Per Serving: Calories: 154; Fat: 5g; Carbs: 3g; Protein: 23g

Corned Beef

Prep Time: 10 minutes
Cook Time: 60 minutes
Servings: 4
Ingredients:
1.8kg beef brisket
2 garlic cloves, peeled and minced

2 yellow onions, peeled and sliced
300g celery, sliced
1 tbsp dried dill
3 bay leaves
4 cinnamon sticks, cut into halves
Black pepper and salt to taste
500ml water
Directions:
1. Take a suitable bowl and stir in beef, add water and cover, let it soak for 2-3 hours. 2. Drain and transfer to the Ninja Foodi. 3. Stir in celery, onions, garlic, bay leaves, dill, cinnamon, dill, salt, pepper and the rest of the water to the Ninja Foodi. 4. Stir and combine it well. 5. Lock and secure the Pressure Lid, then cook on "HI" pressure for 50 minutes. 6. Release pressure naturally over 10 minutes. 7. Transfer meat to cutting board and slice, divide amongst plates and pour the cooking liquid alongside veggies over the servings. 8. Enjoy.
Nutritional Values Per Serving: Calories: 289; Fat: 21g; Carbs: 14g; Protein: 9g

Ninja Foodi Carrot & Pork Stew

Prep Time: 10 minutes
Cook Time: 8 hours
Servings: 4
Ingredients:
450g pork meat, trimmed
1½ onions, sliced thinly
3 carrots, sliced thinly
180ml vegetable stock
Salt and black pepper, to taste
Directions:
1. Add everything in the Ninja Foodi and mix well. Close the unit with Pressure Lid and turn the pressure release valve to VENT position. 2. Select "Slow Cook". 3. Cook at LO for about 8 hours. 4. Open the lid and take out. 5. Serve and enjoy!
Nutritional Values Per Serving: Calories: 465; Fat: 34.8g; Carbs: 21.2g; Protein: 17.1g

Veggies & Beef Stew

Prep Time: 10 minutes
Cook Time: 10 minutes
Servings: 4
Ingredients:
450g beef roast
960ml beef stock
3 garlic cloves, chopped
1 carrot, chopped
2 celery stalks, chopped
2 tomatoes, chopped
½ white onion, chopped
¼ tsp salt
⅛ tsp black pepper
Directions:
1. Stir in listed ingredients to your Ninja Foodi and lock lid, cook on "HI" pressure for 10 minutes. 2. Quick-release pressure. 3. Open the Ninja Foodi's lid and shred the beef using forks. 4. Serve and enjoy.
Nutritional Values Per Serving: Calories: 211; Fat: 7g; Carbs: 2g; Protein: 10g

Beef Bourguignon

Prep Time: 10 minutes
Cook Time: 30 minutes
Servings: 4
Ingredients:
450g stewing steak
225g bacon
5 medium carrots, diced
1 large red onion, peeled and sliced

2 garlic cloves, minced
2 tsp salt
2 tbsp fresh thyme
2 tbsp fresh parsley, chopped
2 tsp ground pepper
120ml beef stock
1 tbsp olive oil
1 tbsp sugar-free maple syrup
Directions:
1. Select "Sear/Sauté" mode at MD on your Ninja Foodi and stir in 1 tbsp of oil, allow the oil to heat up. 2. Pat your beef dry and season it well. 3. Stir in beef into the Ninja Foodi in batches and sauté them until nicely browned up. 4. Slice up the cooked bacon into strips and add the strips to the pot. 5. Add onions as well and brown them. 6. Stir in the rest of the listed ingredients and lock up the lid. 7. Cook for 30 minutes on "HI" pressure. 8. Allow the pressure to release naturally over 10 minutes. Enjoy.
Nutritional Values Per Serving: Calories: 416; Fats: 18g; Carbs: 12g; Protein:27g

Garlicky Pork Chops

Prep Time: 1 hour and 30 minutes
Cook Time: 10 minutes
Servings: 2
Ingredients:
1 tbsp coconut butter
1 tbsp coconut oil
2 tsp cloves garlic, grated
2 tsp parsley, chopped
Black pepper and salt to taste
4 pork chops, sliced into strips
Directions:
1. Combine all the ingredients except the pork strips. Mix well. 2. Marinate the pork in the mixture for 1 hour. Put the pork on the Ninja Foodi basket. 3. Set it inside the cooking pot. Seal with the crisping lid. Choose Air Crisp function. 4. Cook at 205°C/400°F for 10 minutes.
Nutritional Values Per Serving: Calories: 388; Fat: 23.3g; Carbs: 0.5g; Protein: 18.1g

Ninja Foodi Mushroom & Beef Stew

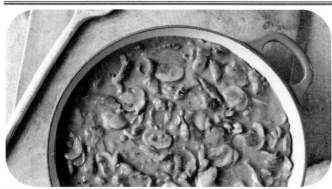

Prep Time: 10 minutes
Cook Time: 8 hours
Servings: 5
Ingredients:
450g beef, chopped
1½ onions, chopped
70g mushrooms, sliced
120ml vegetable stock
Salt and black pepper, to taste
Directions:
1. Add everything in the Ninja Foodi. Close the unit with Pressure Lid and turn the pressure release valve to VENT position. Select "Slow Cook". 2. Close the pressure Lid. 3. Cook for about 8 hours on LO and open the lid. 4. Take out, serve and enjoy!
Nutritional Values Per Serving: Calories: 224; Fat: 6g; Carbs: 11.9g; Protein: 29.8g

Crusted Pork Chops

Prep Time: 30 minutes
Cook Time: 12 minutes
Servings: 6
Ingredients:
Cooking spray
6 pork chops
Black pepper and salt to taste
50g bread crumbs

2 tbsp Parmesan cheese, grated
20g cornflakes, crushed
1-¼ tsp sweet paprika
½ tsp onion powder
½ tsp garlic powder
¼ tsp chilli powder
1 egg, beaten
Directions:
1. Season the pork chops liberally with black pepper and salt. 2. In a suitable bowl, mix the rest of the ingredients except the egg. 3. Beat the egg in a suitable bowl. Dip the pork chops in the egg. 4. Coat the pork with the breading. Place the pork on the Ninja Foodi basket. 5. Close the unit with Crisping Lid and set it to Air Crisp function. 6. Cook at 205°C/400°F for about 12 minutes, flipping halfway through.
Nutritional Values Per Serving: Calories: 310; Fat: 21.3g; Carbs: 8.2g; Protein: 20.3g

Mongolian Beef

Prep Time: 30 minutes
Cook Time: 20 minutes
Servings: 2
Ingredients:
450g flank steak, sliced
30g corn flour
Sauce:
2 tsp vegetable oil
½ tsp ginger, minced
1 tbsp garlic, minced
120ml soy sauce
120ml water
140g brown sweetener
Directions:
1. Coat the beef with corn flour. Put in the Ninja Foodi basket. 2. Seal the crisping lid. Set it to Air Crisp. 3. Cook at 200°C/390°F for about 10 minutes per side. 4. Remove and set aside. Set the Ninja Foodi to sauté. Stir in the vegetable oil. 5. Sauté the ginger and garlic for 1 minute. Stir in the soy sauce, water, and brown sweetener. 6. Pour the prepared sauce on top of the beef.
Nutritional Values Per Serving: Calories: 399; Fat: 11.7g; Carbs: 39g; Protein: 33.7g

Ninja Foodi Beef Casserole

Prep Time: 10 minutes
Cook Time: 8 hours
Servings: 3
Ingredients:
225g beef steak, chopped
90g chopped tomatoes
½ onion, chopped
60ml beef stock
Salt and black pepper, to taste
Directions:
1. Add everything in the Ninja Foodi. Close the unit with Pressure Lid and turn the pressure release valve to VENT position. Select "Slow Cook". 2. Cook for about 8 hours on LO and open the lid. 3. Take out, serve and enjoy!
Nutritional Values Per Serving: Calories: 156; Fat: 4.9g; Carbs: 3g; Protein: 23.8g

Lamb Curry

Prep Time: 1 hour and 30 minutes
Cook Time: 20 minutes
Servings: 6
Ingredients:
675g lamb stew meat, cubed
1 tbsp lime juice
4 cloves garlic, minced
120ml coconut milk
2.5cm piece fresh ginger, grated
Black pepper and salt to taste
1 tbsp coconut oil
350 g diced tomatoes

¾ tsp turmeric
1 tbsp curry powder
1 onion, diced
3 carrots, sliced
Directions:
1. In a suitable bowl, toss the lamb meat in lime juice, garlic, coconut milk, ginger, black pepper and salt. Marinate for 30 minutes. 2. Put the meat with its marinade and the rest of the ingredients in the Ninja Foodi. 3. Mix well. Seal the pot. Set it to Pressure Cook. 4. Cook at "HI" pressure for 20 minutes. 5. Release the pressure naturally. 6. Garnish with chopped coriander. 7. Use freshly squeezed lime juice.
Nutritional Values Per Serving: Calories: 631; Fat: 31.4g; Carbs: 19.7g; Protein: 67.2g

Taco Meatballs

Prep Time: 8 minutes
Cook Time: 11 minutes
Servings: 4
Ingredients:
900g beef mince
1 egg, beaten
1 tsp taco seasoning
1 tbsp sugar-free marinara sauce
1 tsp garlic, minced
½ tsp salt
Directions:
1. Take a suitable mixing bowl and place all the ingredients into the bowl. 2. Stir in all the ingredients into the bowl. Mix together all the ingredients by using a spoon or fingertips. Then make the small size meatballs and put them in a layer in the deluxe reversible rack. 3. Lock with Crisping Lid. 4. Air Crisp the meatballs for 11 minutes at 175°C/350°F. 5. Serve immediately and enjoy.
Nutritional Values Per Serving: Calories: 205; Fat: 12.2g; Carbs: 2.2g; Protein: 19.4g

Beef Enchiladas

Prep Time: 15 minutes
Cook Time: 10-12 minutes
Servings: 4
Ingredients:
450g beef mince
1 packet taco seasoning
4 tortillas
2 diced tomatoes
2 sliced green chilies
180g black beans
1 tbsp olive oil
For Sauce:
1 tbsp red chili sauce
100g Mexican cheese
10g fresh coriander
60g sour cream
Directions:
1. In a medium-size frying pan, take a start by browning the beef mince in olive oil. 2. Then add the taco seasoning to it. Give it a good mix. 3. Once mixed well, put in tomatoes, beans, and chilies. Give it a good mix and set aside. 4. Stir in all the sauce ingredients in a pan and heat the sauce until the cheese melts. Keep stirring until well-thickened. Stuff in the beef batter in the tortillas and wrap them. 5. Place the tortilla wraps in a foil-lined Cooker Cook & Crisp Basket. Pour the prepared sauce on it. 6. Top up with cheese evenly. Air Crisp it for 5 to 8 minutes at 200°C/390°F, until the cheese melts. Enchiladas are ready to be served.
Nutritional Values Per Serving: Calories: 255; Fat: 14.8g; Carbs: 23.1g; Protein: 9.2g

Instant Lamb Steaks

Prep Time: 3 minutes
Cook Time: 7-8 minutes
Servings: 1
Ingredients:
450g lamb steaks
Olive oil
Dry Ingredients:
Salt to taste
Black pepper to taste
1 tsp paprika powder
1 tbsp garlic powder
1 tbsp ginger powder
¼ tsp red chili flakes
1 tsp five-spice powder
1 tsp oregano
Directions:
1. Take out the steaks from the refrigerator and allow them to defrost. 2. Preheat the Ninja Foodi at Air Crisp mode at 200°C/390°F for 5 minutes. Pat dry the lamb steaks and rub them with olive oil. 3. Combine all dry ingredients in a bowl. Press each side of the steaks into the dry mixture then place it in the Cook & Crisp Basket. 4. Air Crisp the lamb sticks at Medium-rare for 7 to 8 minutes. Instant bread meat treatment can be used to check the internal temperature at 60°C. Dish out the steaks and serve!
Nutritional Values Per Serving: Calories: 647; Fat: 43.4g; Carbs: 8.2g; Protein: 1.9g

Mixed Seafood Platter

Prep Time: 9 minutes
Cook Time: 6 minutes
Servings: 6

Ingredients:
450g peeled and devein fresh prawns
450g mussels
1 potato (coarsely cut)
85g fresh corn
340g sausage (5cm pieces)
500 – 750 ml water
2 tbsp old bay seasoning
2 tsp oil flakes
15g fresh chopped parsley
230g butter melted
1 tsp garlic powder

Directions:
1. Add potato, corn, sausages, water, and oil flakes in the Ninja Foodi cooking pot. Give it a good stir. Close the Pressure Lid and turn the valve to Seal position. 2. Now on the High Pressure, cook it for 4 minutes and then do a quick release. 3. Once the timer is completed and pressure is released, open the lid carefully. 4. Now add prawns, mussels, and old bay seasoning. Mix it well and cook it on High Pressure setting in Ninja Foodi for 1 minute. Allow for natural release of pressure for 2 minutes, after 1 minute of cooking in Ninja Foodi High Pressure setting. 5. Then add butter and garlic powder to a small bowl. Mix it well and top up with parsley. Drizzle all over the platter.

Nutritional Values Per Serving: Calories: 521; Fat: 39.9g; Carbs: 22.6g; Protein: 19.3g

Lobster Tail

Prep Time: 4 minutes
Cook Time: 6 minutes
Servings: 2

Ingredients:
4 lobster tails
4 tbsp butter (unsalted)
2 crushed garlic cloves
1 tbsp mixed dried herbs
1 tsp slash parsley
Salt and pepper to taste

Directions:
1. Preheat the Ninja Foodi at 190°C/375°F on the Bake/Roast function for 5 minutes. 2. Meanwhile, cut the lobster using kitchen scissors then cut the centre of the tail until you reach the fins. Do not cut them. Use your fingers to bring the meat up to the top by pulling apart the tail and closing the shell. 3. It should create a butterfly with the meat when you're cutting it so that it can easily be moved to the top of the shell. 4. Melt the butter, add garlic and parsley and mix well in a small bowl. Now drench the lobster tails in a butter mixture. 5. Now place the lobster tail in the Ninja Foodi Cook & Crisp Basket very carefully, and spray olive oil generously. 6. For 5 minutes cook the lobsters, or until the internal temperature of the meat reaches at least 63°C. Lift the lid of the Ninja Foodi once it's done. 7. Take out the golden lobsters and serve!

Nutritional Values Per Serving: Calories: 565; Fat: 36g; Carbs: 0.2g; Protein: 46.3g

Ninja Foodi Parsley Baked Salmon

Prep Time: 10 minutes
Cook Time: 20 minutes
Servings: 3

Ingredients:
450g salmon fillets
¾ tbsp olive oil
1½ tbsp fresh parsley, minced
¼ tsp ginger powder
Salt and black pepper, to taste

Directions:
1. Place salmon fillets in Ninja Foodi and top them with olive oil, parsley, ginger powder, salt, and pepper. Close the unit with Crisping Lid. 2. Select the unit on "Bake/Roast" function. 3. Bake for 20 minutes at 205°C/400°F. 4. Open the lid and take out. 5. Serve and enjoy!

Nutritional Values Per Serving: Calories: 233; Fat: 12.9g; Carbs: 0.6g; Protein: 29.6g

Ninja Foodi Broiled Mahi-Mahi

Prep Time: 10 minutes
Cook Time: 10 minutes
Servings: 2

Ingredients:
225g mahi-mahi fillets
½ tbsp olive oil
2 tbsp fresh orange juice

½ tsp dried thyme
½ tsp cayenne pepper
Salt and black pepper, to taste

Directions:
1. Add everything except mahi-mahi fillets in a large bowl and mix well. 2. Stir in mahi-mahi and toss to coat well. 3. Set aside the mixture for about half an hour and remove the fillets from the bowl. 4. Place them in Ninja Foodi. Close the Crisping Lid and set the Ninja Foodi on Broil function. Adjust the cook time to 10 minutes. 5. Broil for about 10 minutes and open the lid. 6. Dish out and serve hot.

Nutritional Values Per Serving: Calories: 130; Fat: 3.6g; Carbs: 2.1g; Protein: 21.3g

Ninja Foodi Asparagus Scallops

Prep Time: 10 minutes
Cook Time: 10 minutes
Servings: 8

Ingredients:
675g scallops
2 tbsp coconut oil
2 tsp lemon zest, finely grated
40g shallots, chopped
675g asparagus, chopped
2 garlic cloves, minced
2 tbsp fresh lemon juice
2 tbsp fresh rosemary, chopped
Salt and black pepper, to taste

Directions:
1. Add oil in Ninja Foodi and select "Sear/Sauté" mode. Then sauté shallots at MD in it for about 2 minutes. 2. Add in garlic and rosemary and sauté for about 1 minute. 3. Stir in asparagus and lemon zest and cook for about 2 minutes. 4. Add in scallops, lemon juice, salt, and pepper and cook for about 5 minutes. 5. Take out and serve hot.

Nutritional Values Per Serving: Calories: 375; Fat: 6.3g; Carbs: 21.3g; Protein: 59.5g

Ninja Foodi Salmon

Prep Time: 5-6 minutes
Cook Time: 4-5 minutes
Servings: 4
Ingredients:
2 salmon fillets
240ml water
Juice from 1 lemon, about 120ml
Lemon slices
4-5 sprigs of fresh dill (or rosemary)
Salt and pepper to taste
Directions:
1. Pour water and lemon juice into the Ninja Foodi. 2. Add lemon slices and dill. 3. Add the fillets. 4. Add the lemon slices on top of the salmon. 5. Sprinkle with salt and pepper. 6. Secure the Ninja Foodi Pressure Lid. 7. Make sure the valve is set to Seal, cook on High Pressure for 4 minutes. Add an additional minute if the fillet is frozen. 8. Once done, release by turning the valve to Vent (quick release) and then open the lid. 9. Serve the salmon immediately or store in your fridge.
Nutritional Values Per Serving: Calories: 273; Fat: 14g; Carbs: 10g; Protein: 25g

Butter Lime Salmon

Prep Time: 5-6 minutes
Cook Time: 4-5 minutes
Servings: 1
Ingredients
2 salmon fillets
4 tbsp lemon juice
½ tsp lemon zest

1 tsp rosemary
2 fresh dill stalks
Salt and pepper to taste
Directions:
1. Into the Ninja Foodi cooking pot, pour water and lemon juice. 2. Then add lemon zest and dill into it. 3. Into the Ninja Foodi cooking pot, place the deluxe reversible rack. 4. Now place salmon fillets on the lower layer, it is suggested to cut them if they don't fit well in it. 5. Season it by sprinkling salt and pepper on it. Sprinkle rosemary on both sides. 6. Secure the Pressure Lid. 7. Make sure to set the valve on Seal. Cook on High Pressure for 4 minutes. For the frozen fillet add another minute to the cook time. 8. Release the valve on the Vent and then open its lid once done fully. And it's ready to be served instantly or it can also be stored in the freezer!
Nutritional Values Per Serving: Calories: 405; Fat: 15.1g; Carbs: 26g; Protein: 41.7g

Ninja Foodi Ginger Cod

Prep Time: 10 minutes
Cook Time: 20 minutes
Servings: 2
Ingredients:
225g cod fillets
1 tbsp fresh lime juice
½ tbsp fresh ginger, minced
1 tbsp coconut aminos
Salt and black pepper, to taste
Directions:
1. Add lime juice, fresh ginger, coconut aminos, salt, and pepper in a bowl. Mix well. 2. Add cod fillets in the mixture and toss to coat well. 3. Place them in the pot of Ninja Foodi. Close the Crisping Lid and select the "Bake/Roast" function. 4. Bake for about 20 minutes at 160°C/325°F and open the lid. 5. Take out, serve and enjoy!
Nutritional Values Per Serving: Calories: 109; Fat: 1.1g; Carbs: 4.3g; Protein: 20.5g

Prawn Scampi Linguini

Prep Time: 5 minutes
Cook Time: 3 minutes
Servings: 8

Ingredients:
450g linguine
450g (31 to 40) prawns
Salt and pepper (to taste)
3 tbsp olive oil
3 tbsp butter (salted)
2 tbsp garlic (minced)
240ml dry white wine
240ml chicken stock
¼ tsp red pepper flakes
1 lemon (juice of the lemon)
25g parmesan cheese (shredded)

Directions:
1. Turn Ninja Foodi on Sear/Sauté function on HI.
2. Pour in olive oil. 3. Add butter and stir. 4. Add prawns, season with salt and pepper and then stir. 5. Add garlic and juice of one lemon. Be careful not to get the lemon seeds in the pot. 6. Pour in white wine and chicken stock. 7. Add red pepper flakes and stir. 8. Break linguine in half and add in layers, crossing each layer so the pasta does not stick to itself. 9. Once all pasta has been added to the Ninja Foodi cooking pot, press pasta into liquid as much as possible, without stirring. **Do not stir** once you have added the pasta. If you do, your pasta may burn to the bottom of the pot. 10. Put Pressure Lid on Ninja Foodi and move valve to Seal position. 11.

Change Ninja Foodi to Pressure Cook setting on HI for 3 minutes. 12. When timer beeps, quick release pressure by moving valve to Vent position. Turn off the unit. 13. Open Pressure Lid and stir prawns and pasta until its well-combined. Don't panic if your pasta is not 100% cooked. It will continue to cook after you add in the parmesan cheese. 14. Add parmesan cheese and stir. 15. Close the Pressure Lid (**do not turn on**) and let the pasta and sauce continue to combine for about 5 minutes. Stir and Enjoy!!!

Nutritional Values Per Serving: Calories: 396; Fat: 12g; Carbs: 45g; Protein: 21g

Ninja Foodi Salmon with Sweet Potatoes

Prep Time: 10 minutes
Cook Time: 9 hours
Servings: 3

Ingredients:
225g salmon fillets, cubed
180ml chicken stock
¼ tsp ground nutmeg
2 sweet potatoes, sliced thinly
½ onion, chopped
Salt and black pepper, to taste

Directions:
1. Place half of the sweet potatoes in the bottom of the Ninja Foodi and season them with salt and pepper. 2. Place salmon fillets and onion on the top and sprinkle ground nutmeg on it. Pour in the chicken stock. 3. Then, top with remaining sweet potato slices and close the pressure Lid. Turn the pressure release valve to the VENT position. 4. Select "Slow Cook". 5. Cook for about 9 hours at LOP and open the lid. 6. Take out, serve and enjoy!

Nutritional Values Per Serving: Calories: 236; Fat: 5.3g; Carbs: 29.9g; Protein: 17.6g

Beer Battered Fish

Prep Time: 8-10 minutes
Cook Time: 12-15 minutes
Servings: 4
Ingredients:
450g codfish cuts
120g flour
½ tsp baking soda
2 tbsp cornflour
100ml beer
1 beaten egg
Salt as required
¼ tsp Cayenne pepper
1 tbsp vegetable oil
For Flour Mix
90g flour
1 tsp paprika powder
½ tsp black pepper
Directions:
1. Combine flour, cornflour, salt, cayenne pepper, and baking soda in a large bowl. Then add egg and beer, and stir it until it becomes a smooth batter. Let it refrigerate for 20 minutes. 2. Take 85 g flour, paprika, black pepper in a shallow pan. 3. The fish should be at least 1cm thick so that it does not dry out in the Ninja Foodi Cook & Crisp Basket. Take a paper towel and pat dry the codfish cuts. 4. Now coat all sides while dipping the fish into the batter. 5. Allow the egg batter to dip off and again coat it with seasoned flour mix. Any leftover flour can be sprinkled on the fish fillet. 6. Now preheat the Ninja Foodi at Air Crisp Mode at 200°C/390°F for 5 minutes. Spray both sides of the coated fish cuts with vegetable oil and then

place them in the Ninja Foodi Cook & Crisp Basket. Close the Crisping Lid and air crisp them for 12 minutes. 7. During the cooking process, add a little more oil if there is any dryness in the coating!
Nutritional Values Per Serving: Calories: 407; Fat: 6g; Carbs: 26.6g; Protein: 7.3g

Gluten-free Fish Tacos

Prep Time: 8 minutes
Cook Time: 15-17 minutes
Servings: 6
Ingredients:
4 fish fillets
1 tsp paprika powder
½ tsp salt and pepper
1 tsp mixed herbs
6-8 tortillas wrap
For Corn Salsa:
150g soft-cooked corn
180g tomatoes
60g onion
10g chopped coriander
1 tbsp lemon juice
Directions:
1. Take the thawed fish and place it into the Cook & Crisp Basket, then add paprika, salt, and pepper. 2. Spray the Cook & Crisp Basket with olive oil and put it in the Ninja Foodi. 3. Preheat Ninja Foodi at Air Crisp mode at 200°C/390°F for 12 minutes. 4. Meanwhile, combine the ingredients in a bowl for corn salsa. Squeeze a lemon juice on top of corn salsa then remove and flake it apart with a fork once the fish is cooked fully. 5. Now place each tortilla on a plate and add fish and then top it with the corn salsa. Now place each tortilla next to each other in the Ninja Foodi Cook & Crisp Basket. 6. Give it a cooking spray, Air Crisp it at 200°C/390°F for 5 minutes with tongs, remove it carefully, and serve it.
Nutritional Values Per Serving: Calories: 294; Fat: 7.3g; Carbs: 49.2g; Protein: 7g

White Fish with Garlic Lemon Pepper Seasoning

Prep Time: 5 minutes
Cook Time: 10-12 minutes
Servings: 2
Ingredients:
2 whitefish fillets
1 tsp garlic powder
1 tbsp olive oil
2 tbsp lemon pepper seasoning
Salt to taste
2 tbsp fresh chopped coriander
1 lemon (rings)
Directions:
1. Preheat the Ninja Foodi at Air Crisp mode to 200°C/390°F for 5 minutes. 2. Drizzle olive oil on the fillets and season it with garlic powder, lemon pepper seasoning, and salt. Now repeat the step for both the sides. 3. Inside the base of the Ninja Foodi Cook & Crisp Basket, lay the perforated bay paper. Spray the paper lightly with olive oil. 4. Place fish fillets on the paper and add lemon veggies to it. Close the Crisping Lid. 5. Air Crisp it for about 10 to 12 minutes at 200°C/390°F or until fish can be flaked with the help of a fork. Keep in mind the timings depend on how thick the fillet is. 6. Sprinkle chopped parsley and serve it warm with the toasted lemon wedges!
Nutritional Values Per Serving: Calories: 146; Fat: 7.4g; Carbs: 3.7g; Protein: 17.2g

Ninja Foodi Air Crisp Herbed Salmon

Prep Time: 1 minutes
Cook Time: 4-5 minutes
Servings: 6
Ingredients:
200g sizzle fish salmon fillets, I used two, 100g sizzle fish sockeye salmon fillets
1 tsp Herbes de Provence
¼ tsp natural ancient sea salt
¼ tsp black pepper
¼ tsp smoked paprika
2 tbsp olive oil
1 tbsp homemade herb seasoned butter
Directions:
1. Dry your filets with a paper towel and run the surface gently to ensure that there are no bones. 2. Drizzle the olive oil on the fish and rub it in on both sides of the fish. 3. Mix the seasonings and sprinkle them on both sides of the fish. 4. Turn your Air Crisp on 200°C/390°F and set timer for 5 to 8 minutes and cook. I recommend starting with 5 minutes, checking the fish, and increasing the time by one additional minute until it flakes easily with a fork. 5. Melt the seasoned butter for 30 seconds in the microwave and pour it over the fish before eating.
Nutritional Values Per Serving: Calories: 338; Fat: 27g; Carbs: 1g; Protein: 23g

Crumbed Tilapia

Prep Time: 12 minutes
Cook Time: 6 minutes
Servings: 4
Ingredients:
4 frozen tilapia fillets
120g bread crumbs
2 tbsp seafood seasoning
1 egg
Olive oil spray
Salt and pepper
Directions:
1. At 200°C/390°F, preheat the Ninja Foodi Deluxe XL Pressure Cooker at Air Crisp Mode for 5 minutes. 2. To pat dry the fillet, use paper towels and dry the moisture. 3. Add salt and pepper to the egg in a bowl and whisk it well. First, dip the fillet in the whisked egg. 4. Combine bread crumbs with seafood seasoning on a plate and press the fillet from both sides into that mixture to coat generously. 5. Place the fillets in the Ninja Foodi Cook & Crisp Basket and close the lid and cook depending on the thickness of the tilapia and in most cases, 4 minutes have been a good amount of time for a good result. Take out the golden crispy fillets and eat a proteinaceous meal!
Nutritional Values Per Serving: Calories: 212; Fat: 4.5g; Carbs: 15.9g; Protein: 27.5g

Lemon Garlic Scallops

Prep Time: 8-10 minutes
Cook Time: 15-20 minutes
Servings: 2
Ingredients:
450g scallops
½ tsp pepper
½ tsp salt
1 tbsp extra-virgin olive oil
2 tbsp chopped parsley
¼ tsp lemon zest
1 tsp chopped garlic
Directions:
1. Season scallops with pepper and salt. Give the Ninja Foodi Cook & Crisp Basket a generous oil spray. 2. Set the Ninja Foodi at Air Crisp at 200°C/390°F, cook the scallops for about 6 minutes. 3. Now take a small bowl and add oil, parsley, lemon zest, and garlic. 4. Once scallops are seared well, drizzle this mixture over the scallops!
Nutritional Values Per Serving: Calories: 320; Fat: 10.2g; Carbs: 14.4g; Protein: 35.4g

Ninja Foodi Ginger Salmon

Prep Time: 10 minutes
Cook Time: 18 minutes
Servings: 3
Ingredients:
115g salmon fillets
½ tsp fresh ginger, minced
½ tbsp sesame seeds
½ tbsp coconut aminos
½ tbsp fresh lime juice
Salt and black pepper, to taste
Directions:
1. Add all the ingredients to a large bowl and mix well. 2. Dredge salmon fillets in the mixture and transfer them to the cooking pot of Ninja Foodi. Close the Crisping Lid. 3. Select "Bake/Roast" function. 4. Bake for about 18 minutes at 160°C/325°F. 5. Open the Crisping Lid and take out. 6. Serve and enjoy!
Nutritional Values Per Serving: Calories: 64; Fat: 3.1g; Carbs: 1.7g; Protein: 7.7g

Spicy Prawns

Prep Time: 8-10 minutes
Cook Time: 12-15 minutes
Servings: 2
Ingredients:
450g prawns
Salt to taste
Pepper to taste
½ tsp cumin powder
1 tsp coriander powder
½ tsp red chili powder
1 tbsp lemon juice
180g mixed vegetables
Foil (3 to 4 sheets)
Cooking oil spray (olive or coconut)
Directions:
1. Spray the foil sheets with olive oil. Do this on about a maximum of four sheets. 2. Season it up with salt, pepper, red chili powder, cumin, and coriander powder. Pour in some lemon juice and coat all the prawns well. 3. Again, spray another coat of olive oil on foil sheets and put the prawns on the foil. 4. Using the Bake/Roast function, preheat the Ninja Foodi at 190°C/375°F. 5. Cook it using a Bake/Roast function at 190°C/375°F for 13 to 15 minutes. Do this by placing foil sheets in it.
Nutritional Values Per Serving: Calories: 188; Fat: 10g; Carbs: 10.1g; Protein: 37.3g

Fish Skewers

Prep Time: 3 minutes
Cook Time: 8-10 minutes
Servings: 4

Ingredients:
450g frozen fish cubes
6-8 skewers
Salt to taste
Pepper to taste
2 tbsp ginger garlic paste
½ tsp paprika
1 tbsp lemon juice
1 tsp oregano
½ tsp liquid charcoal
1 tbsp olive oil

Directions:
1. Oil spray the Ninja Foodi Cook & Crisp Basket. Combine the fish cubes with all the seasonings in a bowl. Set aside for one to two hours. 2. Align the cubes on the skewers. Now place the fish sticks in an even manner into the Ninja Foodi Cook & Crisp Basket. 3. For 10 minutes, cook at 200°C/390°F in Air Crisp Mode. Flip it if needed and the skewers are ready to be served!

Nutritional Values Per Serving: Calories: 182; Fat: 8.5g; Carbs: 3g; Protein: 23.3g

Bay Crab Legs

Prep Time: 6 minutes
Cook Time: 5-6 minutes
Servings: 1

Ingredients:
450g crab legs
250 – 500ml water
2 tbsp bay seasoning
1 tsp lime juice
1 tbsp garlic infused butter

Directions:
1. Marinate the crab legs with bay seasoning and lime juice. Let it marinate for 30 to 40 minutes. 2. Pour in water inside the Ninja Foodi cooking pot. Any other seasonings can also be used here. Place the rack in Ninja Foodi cooking pot and place the crab legs on top. 3. Seal the Pressure Lid. 4. Cook on High Pressure for 5 minutes. Release the steam by moving the nozzle to Vent quickly, and serve it with garlic-infused butter on top!

Nutritional Values Per Serving: Calories: 272; Fat: 4g; Carbs: 1.1g; Protein: 43.4g

Mexican Rice

Prep Time: 5 minutes
Cook Time: 3 minutes
Serves: 6

Ingredients:
2 tbsp rapeseed or vegetable oil
200g basmati rice
½ green peppers, diced into ½ cm
1 onion (about 110 g), diced into ½ cm
1 carrot, diced into ½ cm
½ red sweet pepper, diced into ½ cm
1 jalapeño pepper, diced into ½ cm
2 tbsp tomato paste
500ml water

Spice blend
1½ tsp fine-grind sea salt
1½ tsp cumin
1½ tsp smoked paprika

Directions:
1. Place the oil in the Ninja Foodi cooking pot. Select Sear/Sauté mode and put it on HI. 2. When the oil is hot, add the rice and sauté for 3–5 minutes, stirring constantly. 3. When the rice starts to brown, add in the vegetables and the spice blend. Stir and sauté for 3 to 5 minutes. Add in the tomato paste and stir to combine. 4. Pour in the water and put the Pressure Lid on. Turn the seal to VENT and select the Steam function for 8 minutes. 5. When finished, remove the lid and stir the rice.

Nutritional Values Per Serving: Calories 178; Fat: 5g; Carbs: 30g; Protein: 3g

Italian Potatoes

Prep Time: 6 minutes
Cook Time: 10-12 minutes
Servings: 4

Ingredients:
4 potatoes
1 tbsp olive oil
2 lemons
½ tsp salt
1 tbsp Italian seasoning
1 tsp mixed herbs

Directions:
1. Wash off the potatoes and cut them into wedges. 2. In the Ninja Foodi, set the cooking pot and then pour in 120ml water. Now add the Ninja Foodi Cook & Crisp Basket into the cooking pot and dump in wedges to it. 3. Preheat Ninja Foodi, Pressure Cook at LO setting for 20 minutes. 4. Pressure Cook potatoes at HI for 4 minutes. 5. Meanwhile, prepare your seasoning mixture by combining Italian seasoning, lemon juice, herbs, salt, and olive oil in a mixing bowl and put its side. 6. Once the potatoes are cooked, release the pressure by setting the valve to vent. After the pressure has been released remove the lid, take 1 tbsp of olive oil, and spread evenly on the potatoes. 7. Now for an additional three to 5 minutes, cook wedges in the Ninja Foodi, until the desired crispiness is achieved. Sprinkle some more seasoning and serve!

Nutritional Values Per Serving: Calories: 70; Fat: 4.1g; Carbs: 11g; Protein: 1.2g

Chives, Beetroot, and Carrots

Prep Time: 5 minutes
Cook Time: 20 minutes
Serves: 4
Ingredients:
450g beetroot, peeled and roughly cubed
450g baby carrots, peeled
Salt and black pepper, to taste
2 tbsp olive oil
1 tbsp chives, minced
Directions:
1. In a bowl, mix the beetroot with the carrots and the other ingredients and toss well. 2. Put the beetroots and carrots in the Ninja Foodi's Cook & Crisp Basket and place it in the Ninja Foodi. Close the Crisping Lid and cook on Air Crisp mode at 200°C/390°F for 20 minutes. Divide between plates and serve.
Nutritional Values Per Serving: Calories 150; Fat: 4.5g; Carbs: 7.3 g; Protein: 3.6g

Garlic Red Sweet Pepper Mix

Prep Time: 5 minutes
Cook Time: 16 minutes
Serves: 4
Ingredients:
450g red sweet peppers, cut into wedges

½ tsp curry powder
110g tomato sauce
Salt and black pepper, to the taste
1 tbsp olive oil
2 garlic cloves, minced
1 tbsp parsley, chopped
Directions:
1. Put the reversible rack in the Ninja Foodi. Place the baking dish on top, and grease it with the oil. 2. Add the peppers, curry powder, and the other ingredients except for the parsley to the dish. Toss to combine. Close the Crisping Lid. Cook them on Bake/Roast mode at 195°C/380°F for 16 minutes. 3. When done, divide between serving plates and serve with the parsley sprinkled on top.
Nutritional Values Per Serving: Calories 150; Fat: 3.5g; Carbs: 3.1g; Protein: 1.2g

Ninja Foodi Brown Rice

Prep Time: 5 minutes
Cook Time: 15 minutes
Serves: 4
Ingredients:
360g brown rice
1 tsp salt
1 tsp cumin
Cooked chicken chunks (optional)
Cooked veggies (optional)
Directions:
1. Add brown rice along with salt and cumin to your Ninja Foodi. 2. Add 550 ml water. Put the Pressure Lid on and turn the steam valve to the Seal position. 3. Select Pressure Cook mode, set it to HI, and adjust the cook time to 15 minutes. 4. When done, allow it to naturally release pressure for 5 minutes, and then release the rest quickly.
Nutritional Values Per Serving: Calories 337; Fat: 12g; Carbs: 73g; Protein: 6g

Cabbage with Carrots

Prep Time: 5 minutes
Cook Time: 20 minutes
Servings: 4
Ingredients:
1 Napa cabbage, shredded
2 carrots, sliced
2 tbsp olive oil
1 red onion, chopped
Black pepper and salt to the taste
2 tbsp sweet paprika
110g tomato sauce
Directions:
1. Set the Ninja Foodi on Sear/Sauté mode at MD, stir in the oil, heat it up, add the onion and sauté for 5 minutes. 2. Add the carrots, the cabbage, and the other ingredients, toss. 3. Put the Ninja Foodi's lid on and cook on HI for 15 minutes. 4. Release the pressure quickly for 5 minutes, divide everything between plates and serve.
Nutritional Values Per Serving: Calories: 140; Fat: 3.4g; Carbs: 1.2g; Protein: 3.5 g

Saucy Kale

Prep Time: 5 minutes
Cook Time: 15 minutes

Servings: 4
Ingredients:
450g kale, torn
2 leeks, sliced
2 tbsp balsamic vinegar
1 tbsp parsley, chopped
Black pepper and salt to the taste
2 shallots, chopped
110g tomato sauce
Directions:
1. In your Ninja Foodi, combine the kale with the leeks and the other ingredients. 2. Put the Ninja Foodi's pressure lid. Turn the pressure release valve to Seal position. Select the unit on Pressure Cook mode and cook on HI for 15 minutes. 3. Release the pressure quickly for 5 minutes, divide the mix between plates and serve.
Nutritional Values Per Serving: Calories: 100; Fat: 2g; Carbs: 3.4g; Protein: 4g

Broccoli Cauliflower

Prep Time: 10 minutes
Cook Time: 15 minutes
Servings: 4
Ingredients:
170g broccoli florets
110g cauliflower florets
2 tbsp lime juice
1 tbsp avocado oil
80g tomato sauce
2 tsp ginger, grated
2 tsp garlic, minced
1 tbsp chives, chopped
Directions:
1. Set the Ninja Foodi on Sear/Sauté mode at MD, stir in the oil, heat it up, add the garlic and the ginger and sauté for 2 minutes. 2. Stir in the broccoli, cauliflower and the rest of the ingredients. 3. Put the Ninja Foodi's lid on and cook on High for 13 minutes. 4. Naturally release the pressure for 10 minutes, divide everything between plates and serve.
Nutritional Values Per Serving: Calories: 118; Fat: 1.5g; Carbs: 4.3g; Protein: 6g

Aubergine with Kale

Prep Time: 5 minutes
Cook Time: 15 minutes
Servings: 4
Ingredients:
Juice of 1 lime
450g aubergine, roughly cubed
20g kale, torn
A pinch of black pepper and salt
½ tsp chilli powder
120ml chicken stock
3 tbsp olive oil
Directions:
1. Set the Ninja Foodi on Sear/Sauté mode, stir in the oil, heat it up, add the aubergine and sauté for 2 minutes at HI. 2. Stir in the kale and the rest of the ingredients. 3. Sear the mixture on Sear/Sauté mode at HI for 13 minutes. 4. Divide the mix between plates and serve.
Nutritional Values Per Serving: Calories: 110; Fat: 3g; Carbs: 4.3g; Protein: 1.1g

Leeks and Carrots

Prep Time: 5 minutes
Cook Time: 15 minutes
Servings: 4
Ingredients:

2 leeks, roughly sliced
2 carrots, sliced
1 tsp ginger powder
1 tsp garlic powder
120ml chicken stock
Black pepper and salt to the taste
2 tbsp lemon juice
2 tbsp olive oil
½ tbsp balsamic vinegar
Directions:
1. In your Ninja Foodi, combine the leeks with the carrots and the other ingredients. Select the unit to Sear/Sauté mode. 2. Sauté on HI for 15 minutes. 3. Divide the mix between plates and serve.
Nutritional Values Per Serving: Calories: 133; Fat: 3.4g; Carbs: 5g; Protein: 2.1g

Creamy Kale

Prep Time: 5 minutes
Cook Time: 15 minutes
Servings: 4
Ingredients:
1 tbsp lemon juice
2 tbsp balsamic vinegar
450g kale, torn
1 tbsp ginger, grated
1 garlic clove, minced
2 tbsp olive oil
240g double cream
A pinch of black pepper and salt
2 tbsp chives, chopped
Directions:
1. Set the Ninja Foodi on Sear/Sauté mode, stir in the oil, heat it up, add the garlic and the ginger and sauté at HI for 2 minutes. 2. Stir in the kale, lemon juice and the other ingredients. 3. Sear the mixture at HI for 13 minutes. 4. When cooked, divide between plates and serve.
Nutritional Values Per Serving: Calories: 130; Fat: 2g; Carbs: 3.4g; Protein: 2g

Potatoes and Lemon Sauce

Prep Time: 5 minutes
Cook Time: 15 minutes
Serves: 4
Ingredients:
450g potatoes, peeled and cut into wedges
1 tbsp fresh dill, chopped
1 tbsp grated lemon zest
½ lemon, juiced
2 tbsp butter, melted
Salt and black pepper, to the taste
Directions:
1. Set the Ninja Foodi to Sear/Sauté mode on MD: HI temperature setting. Add the butter, melt it, then add the potatoes and brown for 5 minutes. 2. Add the lemon zest and the other ingredients. Stir to combine. Close the unit with Crisping Lid. 3. Set the Ninja Foodi to Air Crisp mode and cook at 200°C/390°F for 10 minutes. 4. Divide everything between plates and serve.
Nutritional Values Per Serving: Calories 122; Fat: 3.3g; Carbs: 3g; Protein: 2g

Kale Stir Fry

Prep Time: 5 minutes
Cook Time: 15 minutes
Serves: 4
Ingredients:
450g kale, torn
2 leeks, sliced
2 tbsp balsamic vinegar
1 tbsp fresh parsley, chopped
Salt and black pepper, to the taste
2 shallots, chopped
110g tomato sauce
Directions:
1. In your Ninja Foodi' cooking pot, combine the kale with the leeks and the other ingredients. 2. Put the Pressure Lid on, turn the pressure release valve to Seal position, set the unit to Pressure Cook mode, and cook on HI for 15 minutes. 3. Quick-release the pressure for 5 minutes, divide the mix between plates, and serve.
Nutritional Values Per Serving: Calories 100; Fat: 2g; Carbs: 3.4g; Protein: 4g

Okra Stew

Prep Time: 5 minutes
Cook Time: 12 minutes
Servings: 4
Ingredients:
450g okra, trimmed
2 leeks, sliced
Black pepper and salt to the taste
225g tomato sauce
35g pine nuts, toasted
1 tbsp coriander, chopped
Directions:
1. In your Ninja Foodi, mix the okra with the leeks and the other ingredients except the coriander. 2. Close the unit with Pressure Lid. Select to Pressure Cook mode and cook on HI for 12 minutes. 3. Release the pressure quickly for 5 minutes, divide the okra mix into bowls and serve with the coriander sprinkled on top.
Nutritional Values Per Serving: Calories: 146; Fat: 3g; Carbs: 4g; Protein: 3g

Pomegranate Radish Mix

Prep Time: 5 minutes
Cook Time: 8 minutes
Servings: 4
Ingredients:
450g radishes, roughly cubed
Black pepper and salt to the taste
2 garlic cloves, minced
120ml chicken stock
2 tbsp pomegranate juice
60g pomegranate seeds
Directions:
1. In your Ninja Foodi, combine the radishes with the stock and the other ingredients. Select the unit on Sear/Sauté mode. 2. Cook at HI for 8 minutes. 3. When cooked, divide everything between plates and serve.
Nutritional Values Per Serving: Calories: 133; Fat: 2.3g; Carbs: 2.4g; Protein: 2g

Crispy Balsamic Cabbage

Prep Time: 5 minutes
Cook Time: 15 minutes
Serves: 4
Ingredients:
1 green cabbage head, shredded
2 endives, trimmed and sliced lengthwise

Salt and black pepper, to taste
1 tbsp olive oil
2 shallots, chopped
120ml chicken stock
1 tbsp sweet paprika
1 tbsp balsamic vinegar
Directions:
1. Set the Ninja Foodi to Sear/Sauté mode on MD: HI temperature setting. Add the oil, heat it up, then add the shallots and sauté for 2 minutes. 2. Add the cabbage, endives, and the other ingredients. Stir to combine. 3. Put the Pressure Lid on. Turn the pressure release valve to Seal position. Set to Pressure Cook mode and cook on HI for 13 minutes. 4. Quick-release the pressure for 5 minutes, then divide the mixture between plates and serve.
Nutritional Values Per Serving: Calories 120; Fat: 2g; Carbs: 3.3g; Protein: 4g

Southern Fried Cabbage with Bacon

Prep Time: 5 minutes
Cook Time: 20 minutes
Serves: 4
Ingredients:
300g red cabbage, shredded
60ml veggie stock
A pinch of salt and black pepper
1 tbsp olive oil
245g crushed canned tomatoes
1 lime, grated zest
50g cooked bacon, crumbled
Directions:
1. Put the reversible rack in the Ninja Foodi, add a baking pan, and grease it with the oil. 2. Add the cabbage, the stock, and the other ingredients to the pan. Close the unit with Crisping Lid. 3. Set the Ninja Foodi to Bake/Roast mode at 195°C/380°F for 20 minutes. 4. When done, divide the mixture between plates and serve.
Nutritional Values Per Serving: Calories 144; Fat: 3g; Carbs: 4.5g; Protein: 4.4g

Sweet Peppers Mix

Prep Time: 5 minutes
Cook Time: 16 minutes
Servings: 4
Ingredients:
450g red sweet peppers, cut into wedges
½ tsp curry powder
110g tomato sauce
Black pepper and salt to the taste
1 tbsp olive oil
2 garlic cloves, minced
1 tbsp parsley, chopped
Directions:
1. Put the reversible rack in the Ninja Foodi, add the baking pan inside and grease it with the oil. 2. Add the peppers, curry powder and the other ingredients except for the parsley, toss a bit and 3. Cook on Bake/Roast mode at 195°C/380°F for 16 minutes. 4. Divide cooked peppers between plates and serve with the parsley sprinkled on top.
Nutritional Values Per Serving: Calories: 150; Fat: 3.5g; Carbs: 3.1g; Protein: 1.2g

Minty Radishes

Prep Time: 5 minutes
Cook Time: 15 minutes
Servings: 4

Ingredients:
450g radishes, halved
black pepper and salt
2 tbsp balsamic vinegar
2 tbsp mint, chopped
2 tbsp olive oil
Directions:
1. In your Ninja Foodi cook & crisp basket, combine the radishes with the vinegar and the other ingredients. 2. Cook on Air Crisp mode at 195°C/380°F for 15 minutes. 3. Divide the radishes between plates and serve.
Nutritional Values Per Serving: Calories: 170; Fat: 4.5g; Carbs: 7.4g; Protein: 4.6g

Courgette and Spinach Mix

Prep Time: 5 minutes
Cook Time: 17 minutes
Serves: 4
Ingredients:
2 courgettes, sliced
450g baby spinach
120g tomato sauce
Salt and black pepper
1 tbsp avocado oil
1 red onion, chopped
1 tbsp sweet paprika
½ tsp garlic powder
½ tsp chili powder
Directions:
1. Set the Ninja Foodi to Sear/Sauté mode on MD: HI temperature setting. Add the oil, heat it up, and then add the onion and sauté for 2 minutes. 2. Add the courgettes, spinach, and other ingredients. Stir to combine. Close the Pressure Lid. Turn the pressure release valve to Seal position. 3. Adjust the setting to Pressure Cook mode. Cook on HI for 15 minutes. 4. Quick-release the pressure for 5 minutes, then divide everything between plates and serve.
Nutritional Values Per Serving: Calories 130; Fat: 5.5g; Carbs: 3.3g; Protein: 1g

Low-Carb Italian Wedding Soup

Prep Time: 13 minutes
Cook Time: 15 minutes
Serves: 6

Ingredients:

Meatballs
450g sausage meat
55g parmesan cheese, shredded
20g pork scratchings
60g double cream
1 egg, beaten
½ tbsp Italian seasoning
Salt and pepper, to taste

Soup
1.4L chicken stock
1 garlic, minced
1 tbsp Italian seasoning
1 carrot, chopped
3 green onions, chopped
3 ribs celery, chopped
300g frozen riced cauliflower
75g baby spinach
Parmesan cheese, shredded, for garnish

Directions:
1. Mix the meatball ingredients together in a bowl. Form into 12 meatballs and spread them across the base of the Ninja Foodi cooking pot. Close with the Crisping Lid. 2. Select AIR CRISP mode at 175°C/350°F for 13 minutes.   3. When done, open the lid, pour the stock over the top of the meatballs, and gently stir. 4. Add all the remaining ingredients except the spinach and garnish. 5. Select Pressure Cook mode and close the Pressure Lid. Cook on HI for 15 minutes and then do a quick release. Stir in the spinach.
Nutritional Values Per Serving: Calories 345; Fat: 27.9g; Carbs: 5g; Protein: 18g

Pumpkin Chili

Prep Time: 10 minutes
Cook Time: 4 minutes
Serves: 8

Ingredients:
450g lean beef mince
2 (450g) cans chili beans
1 (410ml) can beef stock
1 (300 g) can diced tomatoes
250g pureed pumpkin
2 tsp pumpkin pie spice
40g yellow or white onion, chopped
1 clove garlic, crushed
1 tsp chili powder
135g ketchup

Toppings (optional)
Shredded cheese
Sour cream
Green onions

Directions:
1. Set the Ninja Foodi to Sear/Sauté mode on MD: HI temperature setting. Add the beef mince and brown it. 2. Drain the beef mince if necessary and then return it to the pot. 3. Add in all the remaining chili ingredients, then stir. 4. Close the Pressure Lid securely, ensuring the steam vent is closed. 5. Select Pressure Cook mode and cook on HI for 4 minutes. 6. Quickly release the steam.
Nutritional Values Per Serving: Calories 345; Fat: 12g; Carbs: 35g; Protein: 25g

Vegetable Soup

Prep Time: 20 minutes
Cook Time: 4 minutes
Serves: 8
Ingredients:
450g turkey mince
1 (400g) can of beef stock
1.7L water
1 (420g) can tomato sauce
165g frozen corn
2 potatoes, halved and quartered
2 large carrots, sliced
2 stalks celery, diced
1 medium tomato, sliced
60g white onion, diced
120ml white cooking wine
½ tsp parsley
150g elbow macaroni
Directions:
1. Set the Ninja Foodi to Sear/Sauté mode on MD temperature setting. Cook the meat in the cooking pot, then add in the remaining ingredients. Then close with the Pressure Lid. Turn the pressure release valve to Seal position. 2. Select Pressure Cook mode. Cover and lock the lid in place. 3. Set to cook on HI for 4 minutes. 4. Quick-release the steam and remove the lid.
Nutritional Values Per Serving: Calories 314; Fat: 13g; Carbs: 26g; Protein: 20g

Black-Eyed Peas

Prep Time: 5 minutes
Cook Time: 35 minutes
Serves: 10
Ingredients:
1 tsp olive oil
120g white onion, chopped
3 garlic cloves
1.4L chicken stock
450g dried black-eyed peas, rinsed
1 fully-cooked smoked turkey leg (about 450-675 g)
1 tsp Creole seasoning
1 bay leaf
Directions:
1. Set the Ninja Foodi to Sear/Sauté mode on MD: HI temperature setting and add the olive oil. 2. When hot, add the onion and garlic. Sauté until translucent and fragrant. 3. Add the chicken stock, black-eyed peas, smoked turkey leg, Creole seasoning, and bay leaf. Stir. 4. Place on the Pressure Lid and seal. Select Pressure Cook mode and cook for 30 minutes on HI. 5. When the pot indicates that the cooking time is over, allow the steam to release naturally for 10 minutes. 6. Open the pot and remove the bay leaf and smoked turkey leg. Use 2 forks to shred the turkey. Return it to the pot. Taste it and add salt and pepper if needed. 7. Serve the black-eyed peas using a slotted spoon.
Nutritional Values Per Serving: Calories 248; Fat: 10.8g; Carbs: 40.7g ; Protein: 2.5g

Chapter 7 Dessert Recipes

Ninja Foodi Blackberry Crumble

Prep Time: 10 minutes
Cook Time: 45 minutes
Servings: 6
Ingredients:
Blackberries Filling:
30g coconut flour
45ml water
30g arrowroot flour
2 tbsp melted butter
55g mashed banana
215g fresh blackberries
¾ tsp baking soda
½ tbsp lemon juice
Crumble Topping
40g oats
55g coconut flour
110g brown sugar, packed
⅛ tsp baking powder
⅛ tsp baking soda
60g butter, softened
Directions:
1. Add all the ingredients for filling except blackberries in a bowl and mix well. 2. Combine the ingredients for crumble topping in another bowl. 3. Arrange blackberries in the bottom of Ninja Foodi cooking pot and pour the filling batter on them. 4. Top with the crumble topping. 5. Close the Crisping Lid and select the unit on "Bake/Roast" function. 6. Bake the crumble for 40 minutes at 150°C/300°F. 7. When cooked, open the lid and take out. 8. Serve and enjoy!
Nutritional Values Per Serving: Calories: 292; Fat: 10.7g; Carbs: 45.7g; Protein: 5.9g

Ninja Foodi Yoghurt Cheesecake

Prep Time: 15 minutes
Cook Time: 30 minutes
Servings: 10
Ingredients:
6 drops liquid stevia
1 tsp vanilla extract
4 egg whites
35g cocoa powder
680g low-fat Greek yoghurt
30g arrowroot powder
Pinch of salt
Crust
30g coconut flour
7 digestive biscuits Granulated sugar
45g brown sugar
1 pinch salt
6 tbsp butter, melted
Directions:
1. Gather all the crust ingredients and dump into the blender. 2. Blend until all the ingredients are well combined and form the sand like consistency. 3. Combine all crust ingredients in a blender and blend until mixture becomes the consistency of damp sand. 4. Dump the crust mixture into the Ninja Foodi cooking pot and pat it down with spatula. 5. Add all the ingredients of cheesecake filling in a large bowl and mix well. 6. Pour the mixture in the springform pan over the top of the crust and place the cooking pot into the unit. 7. Close the Crisping Lid and select the unit on "Bake/Roast" function. 8. Bake the cheesecake for about 30 minutes at 175°C/350°F. 9. When cooked, open the lid and take out. 10. Slice and serve.
Nutritional Values Per Serving: Calories: 236; Fat: 9.3g; Carbs: 35.1g; Protein: 5.9g

Rocky Road Fudge

Prep Time: 5 minutes
Cook Time: 5 hours
Servings: 6
Ingredients:
225g condensed milk
250g chocolate chips
1 tsp vanilla extract
¼ tsp sea salt
65g almonds
60g marshmallows
Directions:
1. On Broil, preheat the Ninja Foodi for 10 minutes with the Cook & Crisp Basket inside. Now add almonds to the Basket and Broil it for 3 to 5 minutes. Take out the almonds and let them cool. 2. Line the square pan with parchment paper, add in chocolate chips and sweetened condensed milk, and then cover it again with the foil. 3. Add 480ml water in the Ninja Foodi cooking pot. Place the pan in Ninja Foodi deluxe reversible rack on the lower position. Close the unit with the Pressure Lid. Turn the pressure release valve to the VENT position. Cook at Steam setting for 5 minutes. 4. Meanwhile, crush the almonds coarsely and cut marshmallows if you're using large ones. 5. Remove the pan from Ninja Foodi and add vanilla, marshmallows, salt, and chopped almonds. Give it a good mix. 6. Then the fudge will start to thicken up as it cools down. Let it cool down for two to four hours in the refrigerator and cut it into bite-size squares!
Nutritional Values Per Serving: Calories: 328; Fat: 18.7g; Carbs: 38.1g; Protein: 7.1g

Double Chocolate Cake

Prep Time: 15 minutes.
Cook Time: 1 hour
Servings: 12
Ingredients:
60g coconut flour
180g sweetener
5 tbsp cacao powder
1 tsp baking powder
½ tsp salt
3 eggs
3 egg yolks
110g butter, melted and cooled
1 tsp vanilla extract
½ tsp liquid stevia
100g 70% dark chocolate chips
480ml hot water
Directions:
1. Grease the Ninja Foodi cooking pot. 2. In a large bowl, stir in the flour, 150g sweetener, 3 tbsp of cacao powder, baking powder, and salt. 3. In a suitable bowl, add the eggs, egg yolks, butter, vanilla extract, and liquid stevia and beat until well combined. 4. Stir in the egg mixture into the flour mixture and mix until just combined. 5. In a small bowl, add hot water, remaining cacao powder and the remaining sweetener and beat until well combined. 6. In the prepared Ninja Foodi's insert, stir in the mixture evenly and top with chocolate chips, followed by the water mixture. 7. Close the Ninja Foodi's lid with a pressure lid. Turn the pressure release valve to the VENT position. Then select "Slow Cook" function. 8. Cook the cake on LO for 3 hours. 9. Transfer the pan onto a wire rack for about 10 minutes. 10. Flip the baked and cooled cake onto the wire rack to cool completely. 11. Cut into desired-sized slices and serve.
Nutritional Values Per Serving: Calories: 169; Fats: 15.4g; Carbs: 4.4g; Proteins: 3.9g

Mocha Cake

Prep Time: 15 minutes.
Cook Time: 3 hours 37 minutes
Servings: 6

Ingredients:
50g 70% dark chocolate, chopped
175g butter, chopped
120g double cream
2 tbsp instant coffee crystals
1 tsp vanilla extract
30g almond flour
20g unsweetened cacao powder
⅛ tsp salt
5 large eggs
125g sweetener

Directions:
1. Grease the Ninja Foodi cooking pot. 2. In a microwave-safe bowl, stir in the chocolate and butter and microwave on High for about 2 minutes or until melted completely, stirring after every 30 seconds. 3. Remove from the microwave and stir well. 4. Set aside to cool. 5. In a small bowl, stir in the double cream, coffee crystals, and vanilla extract and beat until well combined. 6. In a suitable bowl, mix the flour, cacao powder, and salt. 7. In a large bowl, stir in the eggs and with an electric mixer, beat on high speed until slightly thickened. 8. Slowly, stir in the sweetener and beat on high speed until thick and pale yellow. 9. Stir in the chocolate mixture and beat on low speed until well combined. 10. Stir in the dry flour mixture and mix until just combined. 11. Slowly stir in the cream mixture and beat on medium speed until well combined. 12. In the prepared Ninja Foodi's insert, add the mixture. 13. Close the Ninja Foodi's lid with a pressure lid, turn the pressure release valve to VENT position, and select "Slow Cook". 14. Slow Cook on "LO" for 2½-3½ hours. 15. Transfer the pan onto a wire rack for about 10 minutes. 16. Flip the baked and cooled cake onto the wire rack to cool completely. 17. Cut into desired-sized slices and serve.

Nutritional Values Per Serving: Calories: 407; Fats: 39.7g; Carbs: 6.2g; Proteins: 9g

Vanilla Cheesecake

Prep Time: 15 minutes.
Cook Time: 2 hours
Servings: 6

Ingredients:
For Crust:
150g almonds, toasted
1 egg
2 tbsp butter
4-6 drops liquid stevia
For Filling:
450g cream cheese, softened
4 tbsp double cream
2 eggs
1 tbsp coconut flour
1 tsp liquid stevia
1 tsp vanilla extract

Directions:
1. For the crust: in a high-speed food processor, stir in almonds and pulse until a flour-like consistency is achieved. 2. In a suitable bowl, add ground almond, egg, butter, and stevia and mix until well combined. 3. In the bottom of a suitable oval pan, place the crust mixture and press to smooth the top surface, leaving a little room on each side. 4. For the filling: in a suitable bowl, stir in all ingredients and with an immersion blender, blend until well combined. 5. Place the prepared filling mixture over the crust evenly. 6. In the Ninja Foodi's insert, place 240ml water. 7. Carefully set the pan in the Ninja Foodi's insert. 8. Close the Ninja Foodi with a pressure lid, turn the pressure release valve to VENT position, and select "Slow Cook". 9. Cook on "LO" for 2 hours. 10. Place the pan onto a wire rack to cool. 11. Refrigerate to chill for at least 6-8 hours before serving.

Nutritional Values Per Serving: Calories: 446; Fats: 42.9g; Carbs: 7.2g; Proteins: 10.6g

Lemon Cheesecake

Prep Time: 15 minutes.
Cook Time: 4 hours
Servings: 12
Ingredients:
For Crust:
135g almond flour
4 tbsp butter, melted
3 tbsp sugar-free peanut butter
3 tbsp sweetener
1 large egg, beaten
For Filling:
250g ricotta cheese
670g cream cheese, softened
250g sweetener
2 tsp liquid stevia
70g double cream
2 large eggs
3 large egg yolks
1 tbsp fresh lemon juice
1 tbsp vanilla extract
Directions:
1. Grease the Ninja Foodi cooking pot. 2. For crust: in a suitable bowl, add all the ingredients and mix until well combined. 3. In the pot of prepared of Ninja Foodi, place the crust mixture and press to smooth the top surface. 4. With a fork, prick the crust at many places. 5. For filling: in a food processor, stir in the ricotta cheese and pulse until smooth. 6. In a large bowl, add the ricotta, cream cheese, sweetener, and stevia and with an electric mixer, beat over medium speed until smooth. 7. In another bowl, stir in the double cream, eggs, egg yolks, lemon juice, and vanilla extract and beat until well combined. 8. Stir in the egg mixture into cream cheese mixture and beat over medium speed until just combined. 9. Place the prepared filling mixture over the crust evenly. 10. Close the Ninja Foodi with a pressure lid, turn the pressure release valve to VENT position, and select "Slow Cook". 11. Slow Cook on "LO" for 3-4 hours. 12. Place the pan onto a wire rack to cool. 13. Refrigerate to chill for at least 6-8 hours before serving.
Nutritional Values Per Serving: Calories: 410; Fats: 37.9g; Carbs: 6.9g; Proteins: 13g

Raspberry Cobbler

Prep Time: 15 minutes.
Cook Time: 2 hours
Servings: 8
Ingredients:
110g almond flour
40g coconut flour
140g sweetener
1 tsp baking soda
¼ tsp ground cinnamon
⅛ tsp salt
60ml unsweetened coconut milk
2 tbsp coconut oil
1 large egg, beaten lightly
500g fresh raspberries
Directions:
1. Grease the Ninja Foodi cooking pot. 2. In a large bowl, mix together flours, sweetener, baking soda, cinnamon, and salt. 3. In another bowl, stir in the coconut milk, coconut oil and egg and beat until well combined. 4. Add the prepared egg mixture into the flour mixture and mix until just combined. 5. In the pot of the prepared Ninja Foodi, add the mixture evenly and top with raspberries. 6. Close the Ninja Foodi's lid with a pressure lid, turn the pressure release valve to VENT position, and select "Slow Cook". 7. Set on "LO" for 2 hours. 8. Press the "Start/Stop" button to initiate cooking. 9. Place the pan onto a wire rack to cool slightly. 10. Serve warm.
Nutritional Values Per Serving: Calories: 164; Fats: 12.5g; Carbs: 10.9g; Proteins: 4.7

Lime Blueberry Cheesecake

Prep Time: 15 minutes.
Cook Time: 30 minutes
Servings: 6
Ingredients:
1 tsp sweetener
225g cream cheese, softened
80g Ricotta cheese
1 tsp fresh lime zest, grated
2 tbsp fresh lime juice
½ tsp vanilla extract
150g blueberries
2 eggs
2 tbsp sour cream
Directions:
1. In a suitable bowl, stir sweetener and remaining ingredients except for eggs and sour cream and with a hand mixer, beat on high speed until smooth. 2. Stir in the eggs and beat on low speed until well combined, then fold in blueberries. 3. Transfer the mixture into a 12cm greased springform pan evenly. 4. With a piece of foil, cover the pan. 5. In the Ninja Foodi's insert, place 480ml water. 6. Set a "Reversible Rack" in the Ninja Foodi's insert. 7. Place the springform pan over the "Reversible Rack" on the lower position. 8. Close the Ninja Foodi with a pressure lid and place the pressure valve in the "Seal" position. 9. Select "Pressure Cook" mode and set it to "High" for 30 minutes. 10. Once cooked, switch the pressure valve to "Vent" and do a "Natural" release. 11. Place the pan onto a wire rack to cool slightly. 12. Meanwhile, in a small bowl, stir in the sour cream and remaining sweetener and beat until well combined. 13. Spread the cream mixture on the warm cake evenly. 14. Refrigerate for about 6-8 hours before serving.
Nutritional Values Per Serving: Calories: 182; Fats: 16.6g; Carbs: 2.1g; Proteins: 6.4g

Chocolate Brownie Cake

Prep Time: 15 minutes.
Cook Time: 35 minutes.
Servings: 6
Ingredients:
120g 70% dark chocolate chips
115g butter
3 eggs
45g sweetener
1 tsp vanilla extract
Directions:
1. In a microwave-safe bowl, stir in the chocolate chips and butter and microwave for about 1 minute, stirring after every 20 seconds. 2. Remove from the microwave and stir well. 3. Set a "Reversible Rack" in the pot of the Ninja Foodi. 4. Close the Ninja Foodi's lid with a crisping lid and select "Air Crisp". 5. Set its cooking temperature to 175°C/350°F for 5 minutes. 6. Press the "Start/Stop" button to initiate preheating. 7. In a suitable bowl, add the eggs, sweetener, and vanilla extract and blend until light and frothy. 8. Slowly add in the chocolate mixture and beat again until well combined. 9. Add the mixture into a lightly greased springform pan. 10. After preheating, open the Ninja Foodi's lid. 11. Place the springform pan into the Cook & Crisp Basket. 12. Close the Ninja Foodi with a crisping lid and select "Air Crisp". 13. Set its cooking temperature to 175°C/350°F for 35 minutes. 14. Press the "Start/Stop" button to initiate cooking. 15. When cooked, cool the cake completely for about 10 minutes or more. 16. Cut into desired-sized slices and serve.
Nutritional Values Per Serving: Calories: 302; Fats: 28.2g; Carbs: 5.6g; Proteins: 5.6g

Chocolate Blackberry Cake

Prep Time: 15 minutes.
Cook Time: 3 hours
Servings: 10
Ingredients:
200g almond flour
70g unsweetened coconut, shredded
90g sweetener
30g unsweetened protein powder
2 tsp baking soda
¼ tsp salt
4 large eggs
120g double cream
110g unsalted butter, melted
145g fresh blackberries
80g 70% dark chocolate chips
Directions:
1. Grease the Ninja Foodi's insert. 2. In a suitable bowl, mix together the flour, coconut, sweetener protein powder, baking soda and salt. 3. In another large bowl, stir in the eggs, cream, and butter and beat until well combined. 4. Stir in the dry flour mixture and mix until well combined. 5. Fold in the blackberries and chocolate chips. 6. In the prepared Ninja Foodi's insert, add the mixture. 7. Close the Ninja Foodi's lid with a pressure lid, turn the pressure release valve to VENT position, and select "Slow Cook". 8. Slow Cook on "LO" for 3 hours. 9. Transfer the pan onto a wire rack about 10 minutes. 10. Flip the baked and cooled cake onto the wire rack to cool completely. 11. Cut into desired-sized slices and serve.
Nutritional Values Per Serving: Calories: 305; Fats: 27.5g; Carbs: 7.7g; Proteins: 10.6g

Chocolate Walnut Cake

Prep Time: 15 minutes.
Cook Time: 20 minutes
Servings: 6
Ingredients:
3 eggs
110g almond flour
100g sweetener
80g double cream
60g butter softened
20g cacao powder
30g walnuts, chopped
1 tsp baking powder
Directions:
1. In a suitable bowl, mix all the ingredients and with a mixer, beat until fluffy. 2. Add the mixture into a greased Bundt pan. 3. With a piece of foil, cover the pan. 4. In the Ninja Foodi's insert, place 480ml water. 5. Set a "Reversible Rack" in the Ninja Foodi's insert. 6. Place the Bundt pan over the "Reversible Rack" in the lower position. 7. Close the Ninja Foodi with a pressure lid and place the pressure valve to the "Seal" position. 8. Select "Pressure Cook" mode and set it to "HI" for 20 minutes. 9. Press the "Start/Stop" button to initiate cooking. 10. Switch the pressure valve to "Vent" and do a "Quick" release. 11. Place the pan onto a wire rack to cool for about 10 minutes. 12. Flip the baked and cooled cake onto the wire rack to cool completely. 13. Cut into desired-sized slices and serve.
Nutritional Values Per Serving: Calories: 270; Fats: 25.4g; Carbs: 7g; Proteins: 8.9g

Blueberry Buttermilk Cake

Prep Time: 10 minutes
Cook Time: 15-20 minutes
Servings: 8

Ingredients:
8 tbsp unsalted butter
195g sugar (keep 15g aside)
1 egg
1 tsp vanilla
250g plain flour (30g aside)
1 tsp baking powder
¼ tsp salt
120ml buttermilk
300g blueberries

Directions:
1. Beat the butter with 180g sugar for 4 to 5 minutes, until it's light and fluffy. 2. Now add vanilla and egg into it and beat it well. 3. Put in 30g flour, 1 tbsp sugar, and blueberries together in a bowl to coat them and set aside. 4. Mix the remaining flour, salt, and baking powder in another bowl. 5. Add this dry mixture to batter and mix it with a spatula, then add buttermilk. 6. Beat until flour is mixed in and add remaining flour. Now fold in the blueberries and remove the excess flour from the blueberry bowl behind it. 7. Spray the Ninja Foodi cooking pot with rapeseed oil. Pour this batter into the Ninja Foodi. Close the Ninja Foodi with Crisping Lid. Select the unit to Air Crisp function. Air crisp the cake in the Ninja Foodi at 200°C/390°F for 25 minutes. Now select the Start/Stop button for about 15 minutes. Check it with a toothpick and extend the cook time if it's raw. Enjoy!

Nutritional Values Per Serving: Calories: 344; Fat: 12.4g; Carbs: 33.4g; Protein: 4.5g

Crispy Apple Delight

Prep Time: 6 minutes
Cook Time: 10 minutes
Servings: 4

Ingredients:
5 medium-sized apples
120ml water
½ tsp nutmeg powder
1 tsp cinnamon
4 tbsp butter
30g flour
60g rolled oats
50g brown sugar
½ tsp salt
1 tsp maple syrup

Directions:
1. Cut apples in bite sizes and place them on the bottom of your Ninja Foodi cooking pot. 2. Now sprinkle cinnamon, maple syrup, and nutmeg on it. Then pour water over this mixture. 3. Melt butter in a separate bowl then adds flour, brown sugar, butter, oats, and salt to the bowl. Mix it well. 4. Pour this butter mix over the apple layer. 5. Seal the Ninja Foodi with the Pressure Lid and turn the pressure release valve to the Seal position. Cook for 10 minutes on Pressure Cook function at HI setting. Then naturally release pressure for 5 minutes. 6. Lower Ninja Foodi Crisper Lid and let this combination sit for a few minutes before serving!

Nutritional Values Per Serving: Calories: 322; Fat: 12.5g; Carbs: 54.2g; Protein: 2g

Strawberry Crumble

Prep Time: 15 minutes.
Cook Time: 2 hours
Servings: 5
Ingredients:
110g almond flour
2 tbsp butter, melted
10 drops liquid stevia
1kg fresh strawberries, hulled and sliced
1 tbsp butter, chopped
Directions:
1. Lightly, grease the Ninja Foodi cooking pot. 2. In a suitable bowl, stir in the flour, melted butter, and stevia and mix until a crumbly mixture form. 3. In the pot of the prepared Ninja Foodi, place the strawberry slices and dot with chopped butter. 4. Spread the flour mixture on top evenly. 5. Close the Ninja Foodi's lid with a pressure lid. Turn the pressure release valve to VENT position and select "Slow Cook". 6. Cook the crumble on LO for 2 hours. 7. When cooked, cool slightly to serve warm.
Nutritional Values Per Serving: Calories: 233; Fats: 19.2g; Carbs: 10.7g; Proteins: 0.7g

Mini Chocolate Cheesecakes

Prep Time: 15 minutes.
Cook Time: 18 minutes
Servings: 4
Ingredients:
1 egg
220g cream cheese, softened
45g sweetener
1 tbsp powdered peanut butter
¾ tbsp cacao powder
Directions:
1. Grease the Ninja Foodi cooking pot. 2. In a blender, stir in the egg and cream cheese and pulse until smooth. 3. Add the rest of the ingredients and pulse until well combined. 4. Transfer the mixture into 2 (200g) mason jars evenly. 5. In the Ninja Foodi cooking pot, place 240ml water. 6. Set a "Reversible Rack" in the Ninja Foodi's insert. 7. Place the mason jars over the "Reversible Rack". 8. Close the Ninja Foodi's lid with a pressure lid and place the pressure valve in the "Seal" position. 9. Select "Pressure Cook" mode and set it to "HI" for 18 minutes. 10. Press the "Start/Stop" button to initiate cooking. 11. Switch the pressure valve to "Vent" and do a "Natural" release. 12. Open the Ninja Foodi's lid and place the ramekins onto a wire rack to cool. 13. Refrigerate to chill for at least 6-8 hours before serving.
Nutritional Values Per Serving: Calories: 222; Fats: 28.4g; Carbs: 2.9g; Proteins: 6.5g

Mini Vanilla Cheesecakes

Prep Time: 15 minutes.
Cook Time: 10 minutes
Servings: 4

Ingredients:
135g sweetener
2 eggs
1 tsp vanilla extract
½ tsp fresh lemon juice
450g cream cheese, softened
2 tbsp sour cream

Directions:
1. Preheat the Ninja Foodi by selecting Air Crisp function, setting the temperature to 175°C/350°C, and setting time to 5 minutes. Press Start/Stop to begin. 2. In a blender, stir in the sweetener, eggs, vanilla extract, and lemon juice and pulse until smooth. 3. Stir in the cream cheese along with sour cream and pulse until smooth. 4. Stir in the mixture into 5 to 10cm springform pans evenly. 5. Place the pans into the Cook & Crisp Basket. 6. Close the Ninja Foodi's lid with a crisping lid and select "Air Crisp". 7. Cook the cheesecakes at 175°C/350°F for 10 minutes. 8. Place the pans onto a wire rack for 10 minutes. 9. Refrigerator overnight before serving.

Nutritional Values Per Serving: Calories: 436; Fats: 21g; Carbs: 3.2g; Proteins: 13.1g

Banana Bread

Prep Time: 10 minutes
Cook Time: 30 minutes
Servings: 4

Ingredients
2 large ripe bananas
90g plain flour
1 egg
3 tsp brown sugar
2 tsp butter
60g sour cream
½ tsp baking soda
½ tsp salt

Directions:
1. Preheat the Ninja Foodi at Bake/Roast function at 190°C/375°F for 5 minutes. 2. Now grease the mini loaf and set it aside. 3. Take all ingredients in a medium bowl and combine them and stir until combined well. 4. Put the batter evenly in a butter paper-lined loaf pan. Dump the pan in the cooking pot. Close the unit with Crisping Lid and Bake it for 25 to 30 minutes. 5. To check the doneness, make sure that when a toothpick is inserted out from the centre, it is clean. Check the banana bread with a toothpick and serve it warm!

Nutritional Values Per Serving: Calories: 271; Fat: 10.4g; Carbs: 40.8g; Protein: 4.8g

Honey Almond Scones

Prep Time: 5 minutes
Cook Time: 6 minutes
Servings: 6
Ingredients:
250g plain flour
3 tbsp brown sugar
1 egg
1 tsp baking powder
½ tsp salt
240ml milk
1 tsp almond extract
60g butter
Cinnamon to sprinkle
Directions:
1. Combine the dried ingredients in a large bowl. Melt butter in a pan, then adds it to dry ingredients. 2. Now combine all the wet ingredients with the dry ones and stir it. Make sure to not over-work with the dough mixture. 3. Place on parchment paper in Ninja Foodi Cook & Crisp Basket. Scoop out the dough with a rounded spoon on the basket. Set your Ninja Foodi to Air Crisp function and set the temperature at 200°C/390°F for 8 minutes until it's golden brown. 4. Let the cones cool down and then sprinkle a little bit of cinnamon!
Nutritional Values Per Serving: Calories: 267; Fat: 9.9g; Carbs: 37.4g; Protein: 6.5g

Air Crisped Cake

Prep Time: 10 minutes
Cook Time: 20 minutes
Servings: 6
Ingredients:
4 tbsp self-raising flour
7 tbsp butter
240g chocolate chips
3 tbsp sugar
2 eggs
Directions:
1. Melt the butter and chocolate chips. Mix until the chocolate is completely melted. 2. Beat eggs and sugar together in a bowl for 2 minutes. Make sure that sugar is beaten well. Pour this egg mixture into the chocolate mix and fold it to make a smooth batter. 3. Then mix in flour until smooth. Fold it well. 4. Take four oven-safe ramekins, and pour the batter equally in them. Fill it to ¾ of the ramekin and Air Crisp it for 10 minutes at 200°C/390°F in Ninja Foodi. 5. Let it cool for 2 minutes before you flip it onto the plate!
Nutritional Values Per Serving: Calories: 370; Fat: 25.8g; Carbs: 34g; Protein: 5.3g

Ninja Foodi Banana Custard

Prep Time: 10 minutes
Cook Time: 25 minutes
Servings: 4
Ingredients:
1 banana, mashed
240ml almond milk
¼ tsp vanilla extract
2 eggs
Directions:
1. Add all the ingredients in a large bowl and mix well. 2. Pour the batter evenly in custard cups and place them in the Ninja Foodi cooking pot. 3. Close the Crisping Lid and select the unit on "Bake/Roast" function. 4. Bake them for 25 minutes at 175°C/350°F. 5. Open the lid and take out. 6. Serve and enjoy!
Nutritional Values Per Serving: Calories: 196; Fat: 16.6g; Carbs: 10.3g; Protein: 4.5g

Pineapple Chunks

Prep Time: 3 minutes
Cook Time: 10-12 minutes
Servings: 6
Ingredients:
115g melted butter
95g brown sugar
½ tsp cinnamon
1 sliced pineapple
Directions:
1. Combine melted butter, cinnamon, and brown sugar in a low-sided dish. Mix it well. 2. Put in your pineapple pieces to allow it to soak in the flavours for a bit. 3. Add the pineapple pieces in the Ninja Foodi cooking pot. Close the unit with Crisping Lid. Select the Bake/Roast function, and set the temperature to 190°C/375°F. Bake for 12 minutes. 4. Flip the pineapple slices gently halfway through. 5. Serve immediately when ready!
Nutritional Values Per Serving: Calories: 455; Fat: 22.4g; Carbs: 39g; Protein: 4.5g

Conclusion

The Ninja Foodi Smart XL Pressure Cooker Steam Fryer gives you a whole new experience of convenient cooking by bringing a variety of cooking styles into a single appliance. While the Ninja Foodi guarantees effective cooking with minimal supervision, this cookbook ensures that you get the most out of your Ninja Foodi Smart XL Pressure Cooker Steam Fryer by developing its better understanding and by trying all sorts of recipes including breakfasts, poultry, meat, snacks, seafood, and desserts, which are all shared in different chapters of this cookbook. With its single read, all the Ninja Foodi Smart XL Pressure Cooker Steam Fryer beginners can readily learn basic techniques to steam, pressure cook, air fry, bake and cook like a pro.

Appendix 1 Measurement Conversion Chart

WEIGHT EQUIVALENTS

US STANDARD	METRIC (APPROXIMATE)
1 ounce	28 g
2 ounces	57 g
5 ounces	142 g
10 ounces	284 g
15 ounces	425 g
16 ounces (1 pound)	455 g
1.5pounds	680 g
2pounds	907 g

VOLUME EQUIVALENTS (LIQUID)

US STANDARD	US STANDARD (OUNCES)	METRIC (APPROXIMATE)
2 tablespoons	1 fl.oz	30 mL
¼ cup	2 fl.oz	60 mL
½ cup	4 fl.oz	120 mL
1 cup	8 fl.oz	240 mL
1½ cup	12 fl.oz	355 mL
2 cups or 1 pint	16 fl.oz	475 mL
4 cups or 1 quart	32 fl.oz	1 L
1 gallon	128 fl.oz	4 L

VOLUME EQUIVALENTS (DRY)

US STANDARD	METRIC (APPROXIMATE)
⅛ teaspoon	0.5 mL
¼ teaspoon	1 mL
½ teaspoon	2 mL
¾ teaspoon	4 mL
1 teaspoon	5 mL
1 tablespoon	15 mL
¼ cup	59 mL
½ cup	118 mL
¾ cup	177 mL
1 cup	235 mL
2 cups	475 mL
3 cups	700 mL
4 cups	1 L

TEMPERATURES EQUIVALENTS

FAHRENHEIT(F)	CELSIUS(C) (APPROXIMATE)
225 °F	107 °C
250 °F	120 °C
275 °F	135 °C
300 °F	150 °C
325 °F	160 °C
350 °F	180 °C
375 °F	190 °C
400 °F	205 °C
425 °F	220 °C
450 °F	235 °C
475 °F	245 °C
500 °F	260 °C

Appendix 2 Air Fryer Cooking Chart

Chicken	Temp(°F)	Time(min)
Chicken Whole (3.5 lbs)	350	45-60
Chicken Breast (boneless)	380	12-15
Chicken Breast (bone-in)	350	22-25
Chicken Drumsticks	380	23-25
Chicken Thighs (bone-in)	380	23-25
Chicken Tenders	350	8-12
Chicken Wings	380	22-25

Beef	Temp(°F)	Time (min)
Burgers (1/4 Pound)	350	8-12
Filet Mignon (4 oz.)	370	15-20
Flank Steak (1.5 lbs)	400	10-14
Meatballs (1 inch)	380	7-10
London Broil (2.5 lbs.)	400	22-28
Round Roast (4 lbs)	390	45-55
Sirloin Steak (12oz)	390	9-14

Pork & Lamb	Temp(°F)	Time
Bacon	350	8-12
Lamb Chops	400	8-12
Pork Chops (1" boneless)	400	8-10
Pork Loin (2 lbs.)	360	18-21
Rack of Lamb (24-32 oz.)	375	22-25
Ribs	400	10-15
Sausages	380	10-15

Fish & Seafood	Temp(°F)	Time
Calamari	400	4-5
Fish Fillets	400	10-12
Salmon Fillets	350	8-12
Scallops	400	5-7
Shrimp	370	5-7
Lobster Tails	370	5-7
Tuna Steaks	400	7-10

Vegetables	Temp(°F)	Time
Asparagus (1" slices)	400	5
Beets (whole)	400	40
Broccoli Florets	400	6
Brussel Sprouts (halved)	380	12-15
Carrots (1/2" slices)	360	12-15
Cauliflower Florets	400	10-12
Corn on the Cob	390	6-7
Eggplant (1 1/2" cubes)	400	12-15
Green Beans	400	4-6
Kale Leaves	250	12
Mushrooms (1/4" slices)	400	4-5
Onions (pearl)	400	10
Peppers (1" chunks)	380	8-15
Potatoes (whole)	400	30-40
Potatoes (wedges)	390	15-18
Potatoes (1" cubes)	390	12-15
Potatoes (baby, 1.5 lbs.)	400	15
Squash (1" cubes)	390	15
Sweet Potato (whole)	380	30-35
Tomatoes (cherry)	400	5
Zucchini (1/2" sticks)	400	10-12

Frozen Foods	Temp(°F)	Time
Breaded Shrimp	400	8-9
Chicken Burger	360	12
Chicken Nuggets	370	10-12
Chicken Strips	380	12-15
Corn Dogs	400	7-9
Fish Fillets (1-2 lbs.)	400	10-12
Fish Sticks	390	12-15
French Fries	380	12-17
Hash Brown Patties	380	10-12
Meatballs (1-inch)	350	10-12
Mozzarella Sticks (11 oz.)	400	8
Meat Pies (1-2 pies)	370	23-25
Mozzarella Sticks	390	7-9
Onion Rings	400	10-12
Pizza	390	5-10
Tater Tots	380	15-17

Printed in Great Britain
by Amazon

13051341R00047